19 RULES FOR HAPPY RELATIONSHIPS

Simple Strategies for Better Communication, Lasting Love, and Deeper Connection

Debotosh Chatterjee, IRS

BOLD

An imprint of
Srishti Publishers & Distributors

Srishti Publishers & Distributors
A unit of AJR Publishing LLP
212A, Peacock Lane
Shahpur Jat, New Delhi – 110 049
editorial@srishtipublishers.com

First published by Bold,
an imprint of Srishti Publishers & Distributors in 2025

10 9 8 7 6 5 4 3 2 1

Dedicated to the most difficult moments of my life.
They made me realize that a meaningful life is
mostly about managing relationships well!

Contents

Introduction

Relationships form the foundation of human society. It is the way we humans relate to each other that determines the health of a society. From wealth creation to reproduction, the most vital aspects of our society are founded on relationships. However, many of us find it difficult to understand that a relationship – whether parent-child, husband-wife, professional, or friendly – is a living entity. It may not have a physical shape, but it does follow specific rules which living organisms do.

The core of any human relationship is that it should be beneficial to both parties involved. However, the benefits of a relationship are often contingent upon hard work, patience, time, and mental application. Sometimes we tend to waste years in a relationship which makes no sense for us. Sometimes, we may give up on a relationship that could have borne sweet fruits had it been handled the right way.

My endeavour in this book has been to keep a broad scope of discussion. The primary focus shall be on romantic relationships. With the global population comprising a high proportion of young adults, romantic relationships have a significant impact on society as a whole. It is thus essential for these young adults to understand the basics of maintaining romantic relationships with their loved ones.

However, it is not entirely accurate to restrict the scope of relationships to just romantic ones. Thus, relationships with bosses, teachers, parents, and friends have also been discussed in various contexts.

A lack of sound understanding of the ground rules of human relationships can lead to numerous problems, such as lower levels of functioning and a disoriented sense of living. When such issues accumulate at a mass level, there can be a severe impact on the well-being of society. After all, if you are unable to get a grip on how to relate appropriately to different types of human beings in your life, you are unlikely to be successful in personal or professional spheres.

Hence, it shall be my earnest effort to convey the most salient points of human relationships in easy-to-read and straightforward language. As I had intended with my previous book, "8 Things to Do When You Turn 20," this book, too, aims to serve as an appetizer for readers to delve deeper into the subject of relationships.

1.
Magic Person

The concept of "one special person" is firmly rooted in many societies. We are led to believe that there is someone magical who is meant to be our soulmate for life. Arranged marriages, especially in India, have endured and thrived for a long time based on this concept.

Bollywood movies have led us to believe that someone will create magic in our lives. Such magic will be everlasting. We will sing and dance with that magical person and live happily ever after. In India, Hindi cinema of the 1980s, 1990s, and early 2000s largely stereotyped the concept of love and relationships in no uncertain terms.

The concept of finding that magic person is so well-received by youngsters that they are not willing to settle for anyone less than magical. Add to that the age-old belief that loneliness is bad, and you need companionship to survive! Combine the two, and you get a tinderbox filled with FOMO (Fear of Missing Out) and absurd perfectionism. This leads to two things:

1. **FOMO:** Youngsters feel that they need to "be in a relationship" with someone. Most people tend to feel left out if they are unable to participate in the latest dating gossip, and more so if they do not have some substantial relationship "catch" to show for.

2. **Perfectionism:** Someone has to be special and magical. Even with the intention of finding someone to date or be in a romantic relationship with, youngsters feel perplexed by the mediocrity around them. After all, it is actually challenging to find the kind of partners that gossip circles and social media want them to believe. The handsome hunk is not so commonly available, and the heavenly diva is so hard to trace.

This leads to misplaced priorities at an early age. Social media and globalization have joined forces, opening us up to communication in never-before-seen ways. This creates fertile ground for relationship-hunting to begin quite early in life. The codes and priorities of life, however, are not drilled into our minds simultaneously.

Thus, characteristics such as physique, charm, charisma, and outward intelligence are held in high regard by teenagers and those in their early twenties. Priorities change with age, and those in their 30s and 40s generally tend to prioritize income, clarity of thought, and a sense of responsibility, among other things.

Although priorities change with age and time, our past actions cannot be undone. Thus, actions taken by a teenager based on temporary priorities at the age of 19 cannot be undone at the age of 30 just because their priorities have now changed. It is thus essential to develop mental flexibility to understand long-term rules of life as early as possible.

Our parents often emphasize habits such as punctuality and cleanliness right from school days. This is because such habits provide us with long-term benefits. Such emphasis, however, is not available from elders in most families when it comes to relationships. Add to this the frenzy of content on social media, and you get a cauldron of misplaced priorities for the youth.

It is thus essential to clarify this issue sufficiently.

No special person is waiting for you somewhere.

You do not necessarily need to be romantically involved with some outlandish royalty to make your life meaningful.

The hyperbole surrounding dating, one-night stands, and flashy love stories is a product of the commercialization of romance in the 21st century. Actually, there are no rewards for dating the hottest girl in town. Or for having irresponsible sexual encounters with macho males and lascivious females. In fact, most of the fantasizing to get that "dream partner" often turns out to be a waste of time. Simply because real-life partners are not remotely as attractive as we are led to believe, in fact, such dream catches on dating apps have often been reported as elements of elaborate sex rackets!

Now that we have safely addressed our fantasy-driven desires, we can analyze real-life romance and relationships. This is where the obsession to find the "perfect" partner needs to be addressed. Just as we often fumble for an answer to the question, "Who am I?", most of us are equally confused if we are asked the question "What exactly do you want in your romantic partner?" For the sake of discussion, we shall confine ourselves to marriage as the representative relationship.

Most people come up with answers which are commonly available in matrimonial advertisements – educational background, physical traits, family background, pay package, etc. These are traditionally well-known markers which are considered when looking for a suitable partner, especially in marriage. And there is nothing wrong with having particular preferences on these parameters. However, the real problem is that most people are either uninterested or simply too lazy to go deeper than these traditional markers. The real parameters of being a "human being" are often neglected with a gleeful disregard.

Just consider the following: Imagine that you have put forward certain requirements for your prospective bride, and someone fits the bill. You get someone matching the exact criteria that you set. You are on cloud nine, and stop your mental work right there.

You asked for an MBA, and the person has an MBA. But have you discussed with that special person what their future career projections are, and whether they align with yours? If they mention a career track that diverges from your projection in five years, would both of you be mentally prepared to address the issues that arise then? Or would you actually postpone the thinking just for convenience?

You wanted a bride who is slim and fair. Surely, such a person appears to be more presentable to society as is commonly understood. But what purpose does being fair or slim actually serve beyond that? Couldn't you have widened your search significantly by seeking a bride who possesses good communication and social skills?

You may have wanted a groom who has an annual pay package of at least one crore INR. Can you honestly ask yourself whether the figure you have set is merely to attain a certain social status or to have solid financial stability in life? Can you be completely honest with yourself when answering that question?

These are puzzling questions which most people are reluctant to answer. Consequently, they willingly get into relationships without doing the mental groundwork to make them successful over time. This may be due to several reasons, such as laziness, stereotypes, snobbishness, and arrogance. When such a lackadaisical attitude adds up at the societal level, a recipe for substandard social relations is created. Scams and honey traps via dating apps, divorces to extract alimony from the male partner, domestic violence, and dowry demands are all products of a malignant culture that breaks the code of romantic relationships.

It is tough to keep an analytical and open mind at all times. However, if you want a life without messy relationships, the hard work involved in exercising your grey cells is worth the investment.

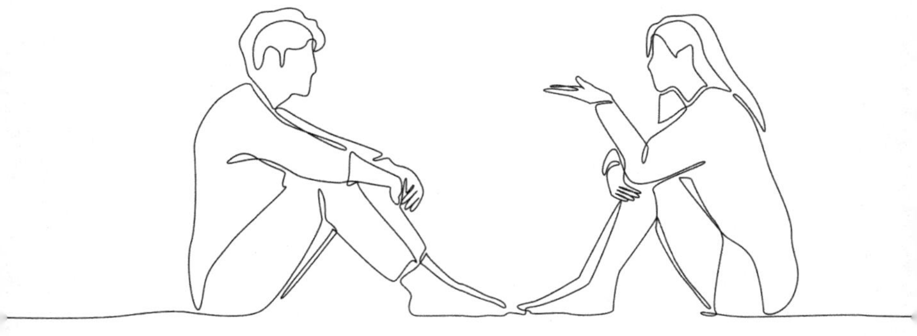

2.
Unique Relationships

A significant aspect of human relationships that goes unnoticed is their uniqueness. Call it laziness, lack of awareness or the absence of common sense, but most of us fail to understand that every relationship with another human being is unique.

There is no dearth of information and know-how on how to manage relationships on the outside. In fact, one can find volumes of information on how to handle life as a couple, what to say when you get home to your wife, what words to use in daily conversations, how to conduct yourself at the dinner table, and so on. However, I have found a general lack of appreciation for the inner dimensions of relationships.

The most important of these less-understood dimensions of relationships is that every relationship is unique, and it needs to be treated on its own merit. While we remain the same person at one end of the relationship, the person at the other end should influence how we handle the particular relationship.

The way you handle your boss should not be the way you handle your parents.

Your relationship with your son should not be a copy of your relationship with your daughter.

Your relationship with a manipulative boyfriend or girlfriend should not overwhelmingly determine how you approach romantic relationships for the rest of your life.

This means that we need to learn the art of distinguishing between one relationship and another as we grow in life. If your father was a drunkard who used to beat up your mother every night, you need to analyze your relationship with your father in its own light. If you have been unlucky enough to have such a father, you have every right to be strict with him and set boundaries which help you create mental peace for yourself.

However, you would be making a grave mistake if you use the same relationship lens to relate to your husband, who is an entirely different person and deserves a different perspective. Thus, if you had set up certain rules with your father because of his characteristics, which determined his relationship with you, you cannot simply apply the same rules to your husband.

Although this concept sounds remarkably simple, it is actually incredibly challenging to implement in daily life. Human beings are social animals driven by habits. They find it very hard to break habits, especially when it comes to relationships.

Chiraunjilal had a difficult childhood in terms of emotional connection and intimacy. He was unfortunate enough to have a narcissistic mother who lacked emotional depth and was extremely unpredictable in terms of warmth and love. One week, she would shower love and affection on him, and the following week, she would be cold and unwelcoming. Chiraunjilal could never understand the roots of the emotional conditionality of his mother.

As a child, he would blame himself for doing things or behaving in ways which may have antagonized his mother. He would always brood over his activities and behaviour, and how his mother would perceive them. This gradually turned him into a chronic approval seeker at a very young age. He became unsure in his actions, tentative in thinking and fragile with his ego.

When he grew up and got married, his perspective on life remained unchanged. He replaced his mother with his wife and kept his old ways intact. He would seek his wife's approval, either directly or indirectly, for even the most trivial issues of daily life. His wife, on the other hand, was an independent woman who cringed at such behaviour. Despite her repeated affirmations of Chiraunjilal's thinking capabilities, she could not change the ways of her husband. He was as unsure at the age of 35 as he was at the age of 10.

This is a case of a person being so overwhelmed by one relationship that they project it onto every relationship in their life. This is damaging not only to the person concerned but also to anyone who comes into their personal or professional circle.

This brings me to the topic of betrayal and heartbreak in relationships, which is so prevalent these days that it has given rise to an industry of romantic gurus. Even though I hold no grudge against these gurus and consultants, I find it slightly bemusing that today's youth trust these relationship gurus more than they trust their own self-awareness and clarity of thought.

One of my close friends was once betrayed by his girlfriend during the early years of college life. He was charismatic, academically brilliant, professionally accomplished, and generous to those around him. However, his heartbreak in college left him extremely jaded in his relationships with women. Even though he tried to be outwardly normal and remain unfazed by such an experience, he would often confide his sorrow behind closed doors and in front of close friends whom he could trust.

He entered several relationships during and after college, but was unable to build anything lasting with any woman. His secret resentment was only covered superficially by a veneer of behaviour and pretensions, but it was always lurking somewhere inside him. Psychologically, he always doubted the women he dated. Such doubts held him back from committing seriously to any relationship. The women he dated generally sensed his doubt sooner or later and left him in the lurch. This further reinforced his resentment towards them. He was stuck in a vicious cycle which was so hard to break.

Needless to say, my friend fell prey to the fallacy of painting every romantic relationship with the same brush. This is a widespread phenomenon among today's youth. Unsolved psychological issues are damaging in the long run. It has become such a social evil that betrayed lovers have gone to the extent of acid attacks and murders of their ex-partners.

Inability to grow beyond certain kinds of relationships – such as those with abusive parents, manipulative partner, devilish boss, unfaithful girlfriend – is more a result of lack of self-awareness than anything else. I must clarify here that this does not mean that such relationships are easy to tackle. However, people's (and mainly the youth's) reluctance to cultivate their self-awareness through time-tested methods (such as reading, observing, and comprehending) is something that needs addressing.

The thumb rule for creating happy relationships is to have an open and flexible mind, which can handle setbacks and also allow the influx of new experiences in life.

3.
Understanding Your Own Nature

Relationships are all about relating to another human being. That's true. However, most people tend to view relationships as a one-way street. This makes the person at the other end of the relationship the determining factor in the success and longevity of the relationship. Most romantic relationships tend to falter on this very concept.

The prevalent concept of finding a suitable partner is that we zero in on the qualities and characteristics which we find attractive. Based on these attraction factors, we seek the most suitable partner. This can happen in casual dating, when looking for partners for arranged marriage, and even when choosing team members in the office.

The fallacy in this concept is that it is highly externalized. You are essentially looking for someone who possesses some of the qualities that are important to you.

Some may be looking for a partner who is fair and handsome. Some may seek intellectual depth. Some may find beauty in family pedigree. Some may be obsessed with money.

There may be one or more of these factors, which can be combined, ultimately determining what we tend to look for in a partner. A glance at the matrimonial columns of popular newspapers across the world tells that such factors are predictable to a large extent.

The critical missing factor is self-assessment. Most of us are lazy enough to dismiss the suggestion. Look around – how many people can actually write 500 words about themselves? On the contrary, the list of demands people have from a potential partner is mostly endless.

Why so? Because of an aversion to doing basic self-assessment. This is one of the primary reasons why people suffer in bad relationships throughout their lives.

To understand who would be a suitable partner for any purpose – romantic, professional, or friendly – you first need to be thorough about yourself. This means you need to be fully aware of some aspects of your own life. For the sake of discussion, consider the following aspects of life and how carefully you understand them:

1. **Your lifestyle:** Are you very particular when it comes to your daily routine, or are you flexible enough to accommodate someone who may go to bed later than you do?
2. **Your value systems:** Are you a stickler to rules, or are you okay with bending them from time to time? If you are open to being flexible, what are your boundaries when it comes to your values? Would you be okay if your partner insists on lying to family members for the sake of fake peace, or would that infuriate you? THINK!
3. **Your food habits:** This is a significant issue which often goes unnoticed in the initial stages of relationships. However, when you find that you have to live with someone who insists on having non-vegetarian food at least four times a week, while you abhor the smell of fish or chicken, issues are bound to arise.
4. **Your cultural upbringing:** Different cultures produce different human beings. While the external factors, such

as language, caste, and skin colour, may remain the same, the cultural background can create issues down the line. Growing up in a family where fraudulent behaviour, such as professional misconduct and debauchery in personal life, is considered acceptable and brushed under the carpet is enormously different from growing up in a family where ethics are always held in high regard.

5. **Your professional choices:** More often than not, we consider our career and professional decisions to be etched in stone, and expect the other side to compromise wherever possible. If the initial attractive factors are present, we tend to move forward in relationships where issues related to professional choices are likely to arise. If such problems are not discussed in the early stages, the disharmony grows with time. Can a criminal lawyer known for defending corrupt people be happily married to an upright cop?

This is just a rudimentary list of factors which we must consider and assess about ourselves first. You can continue to add to the list based on your own circumstances. A football fan who spends weekends zealously watching the sport on TV will have a hard time putting up with a partner who hates football.

It is thus essential to spend as much time as possible trying to understand oneself first. The better the assessment, the more likely you are to succeed in your relationships.

Honest self-assessment is rare because it is a challenging task. Most people prefer to hide their deficiencies by pointing out a list of problems in their partner.

Vivek frequently argues with his wife, Kavya, because he believes he is late for work due to Kavya's carelessness at home.

He rarely acknowledges the fact that he is a compulsive late riser in the morning who wastes time scrolling through social media at night.

Arya thinks her boyfriend, Kabir, never understands the nature of her troubled relationship with her parents. She laments the lack of support from Kabir on various issues concerning her parents. She never admits to the fact that her communication with both Kabir and her parents is extremely fuzzy and difficult to understand. Kabir is perennially confused because Kavya's words and actions vis-à-vis her parents do not match.

She criticizes her mother on almost everything and yet prefers to share intimate secrets (personal and professional) with her instead of Kabir.

She is forever complaining about how mean and disgusting her cousins are, but spends entire weekends with them without even telling Kabir.

Kabir is confused about what to trust, but Arya does not care about honest self-assessment.

In relationships where the "intent" to be honest with oneself is missing, confusion and mental agony are always present. Looking inwards is very difficult because we are scared of the demons inside us. Instead, the easier path is to blame the other side and go carefree. Such lazy attitudes only lead to substandard relationships, which generate scarce growth in the long term.

4.
Contrasting Value Systems

One of the major fallacies in the thought process of most young adults is that they consider relationships to be isolated entities. They are not. Human relationships are as organic as human beings. They are created over years of conditioning by social, cultural, and psychological forces.

When two adults decide to enter an intimate relationship, they are actually combining two systems of thinking and living into one. While a few factors of attraction are enough to signal mutual interest, there is always the risk of ignoring noticeable differences that can emerge later on. Let's understand this point using the example of Vrinda and Shravan.

Vrinda and Shravan were introduced to each other by a mutual friend. They liked each other because of shared interests, such as similar food preferences and living habits, as well as intellectual synchronicity and physical compatibility. Quite soon, they hit off like a couple on song. Both were inseparable. They felt that it was a match made in heaven. Everything appeared so smooth that they decided to get hitched. That was when reality hit them hard.

Even though both Vrinda and Shravan had apparently similar upbringings in terms of caste, language, food habits, and lifestyle, they found massive differences in their family cultures and value systems. This difference became evident once their union was formalized in the form of marriage, allowing the two contrasting value systems to come into direct contact.

Vrinda belonged to a culture that condoned chronic lying. Shravan and his family found it difficult to tolerate her incessant misrepresentations. Vrinda, who was used to such lying while growing up, found it puzzling to see her husband and in-laws react awkwardly to her behaviour.

Besides, Vrinda's upbringing was such that she was accustomed to seeing her parents brush aside essential issues to avoid difficult discussions. This culture was diametrically opposite to Shravan's life, in which he grew up seeing his parents struggle hard to resolve family issues, often involving verbal altercations.

Shravan grew up in a culture where pretending was not okay when it came to life-threatening issues. Vrinda was accustomed to seeing her mother adopt a permanent air of nonchalance towards almost everything.

Clearly, the initial factors of attraction found it challenging to overcome years of cultural and systemic conditioning. Such a clash of value systems only leads to deterioration in the quality of life, with both parties in the relationship perennially wondering where they went wrong. Actually, they didn't, but their systems did!

As we grow up and start interacting with people, it is essential to understand the various value systems around us. These value systems create driving forces which determine a person's behaviour. Thus, a mature adult who seeks out fulfilling relationships must first endeavour to clearly identify the value system to which they belong and the ones that they can accommodate.

Let us understand this point with the example of Kush and Bipasha.

Kush belongs to a household which has historically produced freedom fighters. He enters into a relationship with Bipasha, who comes from a family of businessmen and politicians. In such a case, conflict and tensions may appear even with no fault of Kush or Bipasha.

Bipasha's parents have the habit of making cash deposits in her bank account from time to time. Kush is not comfortable with this, as he is unsure about the financial credentials of Bipasha's parents. He thinks that he may be silently becoming party to black money transactions. Bipasha finds nothing wrong with her parents' actions, as she has been accustomed to them since childhood. She cannot understand Kush's concerns because her background systems are developed accordingly.

Tensions build up between the two on this issue, but a resolution is unlikely as long as Kush and Bipasha remain entrenched in their respective background systems of thought.

The problem with value systems is that most people struggle to articulate them properly. Ask any person on the street about the chances of the ruling political party in the upcoming elections, and they will give you an elaborate answer. Ask them about the elements in their value system and why they hold these values. They are most likely going to be confused. Most of us will struggle to correctly answer the question, "Who am I?" because a significant component of the answer consists of the value system. Try to ask yourself:

1. Am I a person of integrity? If so, what does integrity mean? If I believe I possess integrity, would I be willing to tolerate fundamentally dishonest people? To what extent can I tolerate my own spouse if they are okay with dishonesty, while I claim to be a person of integrity?
2. Am I a religious person? Is my religiosity deeply ingrained or merely superficial? Would I be able to relate to people who take religiosity for a joke?

3. Am I an objective person who relies on facts and logic for decision-making? If so, how do I deal with problematic in-laws who have fuzzy thinking and behaviour patterns?

When you start asking and answering such questions on your own, you will get a fair understanding of what your value system consists of. This is the first hurdle, which is difficult to cross because most of us are okay with being lazy in this aspect of life. To cross this hurdle and ask another person in a relationship with you about their value systems is another herculean task. It entails arduous work, and we feel better off in the sea of vagueness around us.

However, such lazy thinking is a recipe for disaster in society in the long term. Suppose people cannot figure out their value systems at the individual level. Would it be possible for organizations, societies and nations as a whole to be clear with their value systems? Can you have a nation of hardworking, honest people and take pride in such a culture if the people themselves are not clear about being honest and hardworking? Clearly not; this has resulted in the fall of great nations and civilisations over time.

Twenty-first-century youth, however, always have the option to seek out independent thinking. You are no longer bound by what your forefathers thought about a particular issue. You are entitled to have a mind of your own, which is to be used for self-betterment. In fact, it is the generational change in thought process that has led to changes across the globe on issues like slavery, child labour, women's right to vote, etc.

Being an independent thinker allows you to befriend and relate with other such thinkers who are not weighed down by their narrow thought process. It is always advisable for young people to learn and prioritize independent thinking as early as possible.

The term "independent thinking" may sound too heavy, but it is astonishingly simple. It means learning to use your senses and thoughts to figure out what is best for you. Just because your parents "taught" you to lie does not mean you should take up the habit without thinking. On the other hand, if someone in your family has been a true luminary in their field, you should seek their advice even if others do not like them.

Independent thinking is all about "learning and implementing" what is best for oneself and society. The best relationships happen between independent thinkers who learn to collaborate on principles in mutual interest.

5.
Love is Subjective

Love is one of the most frequently used and misused words in the English dictionary.

People having extra-marital affairs have no problem saying that they still love their spouse.

Incompetent parents who use their children as trophies claim that their actions stem from love for their children.

Friends-with-benefits who meet on dating apps can easily say "I love you" to each other while the fun lasts.

It is so easy to use the four-letter word that virtually anybody can use as a general ointment for relationships. However, getting down to the specifics of love is quite tricky. This is why most people who profess love towards their loved ones at the drop of a hat find it irritating and problematic when asked to "elaborate" or "discuss" the "how/why/what" of their love.

Love is a profoundly strong emotion which holds human society together. However, there is no universal language that accounts for the expression of love. This is quite different from the other well-known emotions, which have established expressions.

Anger leads to rage and destruction. Most people have no problems expressing anger. They may shout, fight, abuse and whatnot.

Fear is a strong emotion which holds people back from normal behaviour. If you are scared of your examinations at school or a job interview, people around you can sense it from your demeanour and verbal/non-verbal expressions.

Happiness and joy are other emotions that are well recognized because they are expressed in known ways. If you are happy, you are likely to be ebullient, charged up, or excited. People around you can instinctively know that you are happy even if you do not say so.

Love is different. Mainly because its expression is not codified, it is somewhat mysterious and vague, and thus open to misuse by criminals for their own benefit.

Shiva and Parvati have been married for a few years. Before their marriage, they had been in a committed relationship for three years. When they were dating, the match seemed perfect. Things moved so smoothly that they decided to get hitched, even though Parvati's parents had massive unresolved ego issues with Shiva.

The relationship began to take a more realistic turn after they got married. Once the mushy season was over, it was down to the brass tacks and the grind of daily life. This is when both parties felt the acute lack of synchronicity in their definition of love.

Shiva often interpreted his iron-willed commitment and protectiveness towards Parvati as proof enough of his love. He would act tough against anyone or anything that threatened his spouse. However, he was not among the soft types and had an imposing personality. At times, his steadfastness was taken as rudeness by many people, including Parvati. Shiva, true to his own nature, expected Parvati to be tough as well. Whenever Parvati appeared submissive and meek to anyone, including her own parents, Shiva would interpret it as Parvati prioritizing her people-pleasing attitude over her love for Shiva.

For Parvati, love had a different dimension. She expected Shiva to compliment her on the small things of daily life. If she brought home a lamp for the study table to decorate the house, she expected Shiva to appreciate it verbally. The absence of such appreciation (Shiva being a hard nut in his own way!) would make her think of Shiva as a cold and unloving person. Parvati expected Shiva to have a submissive demeanour towards her family members. Shiva, himself battling ego issues with Parvati's parents, had no intention of acceding to such expectations. In fact, because of his no-nonsense nature, he clearly said no to having any relationship with Parvati's parents unless the ego issues were resolved.

Needless to say, even though both Shiva and Parvati "felt love" towards each other, they found it difficult to reconcile with the ground realities. They interpreted each other's actions in such different lights that it became difficult to ascertain how real the love actually was.

This is why love is such a tricky emotion. It tends to create ambiguity and keeps people bonded together even when circumstances seem extremely hostile. However, the overpowering nature of love confuses people when their thoughts and reality diverge, as is the case with Shiva and Parvati.

It is therefore necessary for any romantic relationship to work out a mutually acceptable definition of love. The specifics must be so precise that expressions and behaviour of either partner reinforce the emotion instead of creating fuzziness in the mind. So, Shiva and Parvati need to have a detailed conversation about what exactly they want from each other. It would definitely not be possible for either of them to agree to all such expectations of the partner completely.

So, while Shiva may have reservations about appearing submissive to Parvati's parents, he can agree to a monthly visit to her parents' place for formality. Parvati, on her part, should take up some of Shiva's tough stands on various issues (including ego tussle with her parents) and express her support from time to time.

A harmonious middle ground thus becomes a critical bulwark against degradation in relationships. The concept of the middle ground has been advocated by no less than a towering personality like Gautam Buddha. Aristotle was the proponent of "the Golden Mean is the Golden Rule". Once partners realize that they have reached a middle ground in the relationship, they will soon feel the benefits that are missing from the relationship.

It is the process of reaching the critical middle ground on wide-ranging issues over time that becomes a test of love. You must be ready to put in the hard yards and make sacrifices over time for a person you claim to love. Such hard work, of course, cannot be a one-sided affair, and the other person needs to be equally serious in their efforts. This can happen when partners have a consensual urge and willingness to find common ground on critical life issues.

However, most people fail to reach the middle ground either because they fail to understand the benefits of such a "golden mean" or because they are too lazy to work towards that point. For example, if any of your daily habits is a cause of discord with your spouse, you need to work hard to address the concern. If there is genuine love in the relationship, it motivates you to do such work. Otherwise, people are content in keeping relationships at suboptimal levels.

What is colloquially known as "compromise" is actually one of the best ways to sustain human relationships, in a way that benefits both and exploits none. It sounds relatively easy, but implementing and maintaining it over long periods of time is incredibly difficult.

6.

Trust: Non-Negotiable

TRUST: This is yet another word that is often used with such thoughtlessness that it has lost much of its innate salience. Since there is no universally agreed-upon definition of trust, people tend to take liberties when creating their own version. There are several theoretical definitions for the word "trust," but it is the practical aspect of the word that causes concern in the context of relationships. Thus, instead of repeating the theoretical elements of trust, let us understand it from a convenient point of view.

Let us consider the relationship of a husband-wife for better understanding. Trust is like an invisible key to the complicated code that defines the relationship. The man and the woman are two distinct human beings, with different minds, cultural upbringings, backgrounds, professions, habits, and so on. Even though they are going to converge on multiple aspects (such as food habits and financial discipline), it is not possible to have a relationship between two exact copycats.

The differences create a need for two individuals to reach a mutually beneficial compromise, thereby fostering a meaningful relationship that is mutually beneficial to both parties. However, it is simply impossible to physically pen down any such "Charter of the Common Ground" when two persons form a relationship.

Yes, the basics are always visible – daily routine, future goals, etc., but one simply cannot predict life with another person with pinpoint accuracy on a 24/7 basis.

For example, a couple may agree on a daily routine that involves breakfast at 8:00 a.m. every day. However, what is the guarantee that either of the spouses will not break the routine on certain Mondays and Thursdays at random?

If the mutual consensus is to keep a spare key for the main entrance of the house under the flower pot, what guarantee is there that someone will not put it somewhere else?

The most fundamental issue would be – what if the husband or the wife suddenly "decide" to like or love someone else? How is the partner supposed to respond in such a situation, or even live with that person daily, without the assurance that they would not suddenly run away with someone else?

There can be an infinitely long list of such issues which can create a whole lot of chaos between a couple. So, how do most couples typically steer clear of such turmoil and survive?

The answer is TRUST.

Trust is the bi-directional key to the relationship. It opens the door on both sides. If both partners can trust each other, they can be assured that such chaotic issues, as highlighted above, are very unlikely to arise. More importantly, trust provides a certain degree of control in relationships which are otherwise susceptible to external influence and whose "micro" aspects are too complex to decipher satisfactorily.

So, if you trust your wife, you can be sure that she will not steal money from your cupboard. That will help you relax whenever you are not at home. Imagine what would happen if you were to share your home with someone whose disposition towards your money is doubtful.

A similar understanding can be gained in the context of professional relationships. If your boss does not trust you, he is unlikely to give you the assignments that can help you earn the reputation that you need to surge ahead in your career. A manager of any kind of team – from a company CEO to a nation's Prime Minister – would thus prefer to surround themself at all times with people they can trust. This makes their job much easier than if they were to handle people whom they do not fully understand. It is precisely because of "trust" and its critical role in relationships that we can notice a flurry of changes in key managerial positions whenever a significant change happens at the top levels of an organization or a country. Bureaucratic reshuffles worldwide are based on the premise of trust.

The trust key, if we may call it so, is unique to a relationship. This means that the same key does not work for every door. The trust factors that work at your home may not necessarily work with your boss – they are different relationships with different keys. Therefore, the way you develop and maintain trust with your boss will require different dynamics from those you use when managing trust with your partner.

Now that we have sufficiently addressed the "what" of trust, it is time to explore the question of "how". After all, if trust is the key to establishing predictability and stability in relationships, it is essential to work towards "generating" the requisite trust and becoming "trustworthy". This is where the hard work comes in, making trust a much more difficult proposition than it initially sounds.

Trust in a relationship between two people is based on an imaginary "trust-bank", and either side acts as the trustee of the bank. You can consider the relationships between husband and wife, boss and employee, politician and adviser, friends, and so on in the same light. Both sides in the relationship are protectors of the trust bank, which they have to build over time. The bank fills up over time through trustworthy actions, emotions, and events from both sides. The bank provides compound interest on its deposits, which means that if the deposits are consistently added over long periods, the returns are substantial. At the initial stages of any relationship, the imaginary trust bank is only slightly full and needs deposits from both sides.

Trust is reciprocal. This means that when the person at the other end of the relationship performs an act of trust, you must reciprocate with something equally trustworthy in the future. If such reciprocity is not present from one side on multiple occasions, the trust in the bank begins to erode. Just as the growth of trust compounds over time, its erosion is also subject to compounding.

If too many liberties are taken by either side in a relationship, trust erodes quickly. If you catch your partner texting their work friend late at night almost every day, and you get no clear answers on confronting them, it's a case of your partner taking liberal withdrawals from the trust bank. This will not be sustainable in the long run. Similarly, if you are tagged as a habitual offender prone to lapses in professional conduct, your relationship with the employer is likely to deteriorate over time.

Sometimes, there can be robberies at the trust bank, which shatters the very foundation of the relationship. This can happen when severe lapses are found. A sentry who is charged with the duty of protecting people commits an unpardonable offence against the trust placed in them by their employer (a sovereign government), if they are found guilty of extorting money from the very people they are supposed to protect. If you discover that your partner has been secretly getting physically intimate with their office colleague, it becomes a severe attack on the trust bank of your marriage.

Becoming a trustworthy person generally requires a fundamental element: your words should consistently match your actions. If you say something and then end up doing something else as a matter of habit, the society around you is very likely to brand you as "untrustworthy". That would make you a suspect case in multiple domains – at home, in social circles, at the office, etc.

Pathological and habitual lying is yet another trademark of untrustworthy people. One should steer clear of such characters at all costs. When people consistently lie, it reveals their lack of dependability. Such people cannot be trusted with any trust bank. They rarely reciprocate the deposits you make into the bank, and are most likely to rob the bank which gets built based on your deposits. These are the "manipulative" people that we find around us, whom we need to be cautious about.

The thumb rule of most successful people across the globe and across the generations from Ashoka, Alexander to Steve Jobs, Michael Phelps and Sachin Tendulkar is to be surrounded by trustworthy people. If you waste time with untrustworthy people, you are doing yourself a great disservice.

Living with trustworthy people and being reliable is one of the most significant components of success in human society, a principle that has been true since time immemorial.

A bond between two people begins with love and attraction, but it is sustained by trust. Nothing is exciting about trust – it does not evoke the hormones that love and lust do. It isn't easy to generate, and it is extremely painstaking to sustain over long periods. Trust built by years of hard work can get undone within minutes or by a single act of betrayal.

7.
Honesty and Empathy

In the book so far, we have learnt how important it is to have clarity about the people with whom we intend to relate. We have analyzed the impact of unhealthy relationships in our lives and discussed ways to enter into the right kind of relationship that suits us and improves our lives in the long run. We have seen the importance of love and trust in making relationships successful.

This provides us with the necessary background to understand the finer aspects of human relationships. In this context, we will examine the roles of honesty and empathy in making relationships successful.

Honesty as a trait has already been touched upon in the chapter on trust. Honesty is a simple virtue which creates the most potent results. Honest individuals tend to form frank relationships, which often develop over time. Honesty can make relationships more straightforward to handle if both parties agree to uphold it. Honesty as a virtue has been debated and discussed since time immemorial. Greek philosophers, such as Socrates and Plato, have produced memorable commentaries on its role in human civilisation as a whole. However, a detailed discussion on honesty is beyond the scope of this book, and we are more concerned with its practical aspects in relation to human relationships.

In layperson's terms, honesty implies an emphasis on truth

and lack of deception. While such a rudimentary definition of honesty may not encompass all its aspects, it effectively conveys why honesty is crucial for relationships to succeed. If both sides in a relationship are honest and have a consensus to steer clear of deception, it usually leads to a sense of security. If you know that you are dealing with someone who actually is what he claims to be, then much of your mental energy can be spared from thinking about their ulterior motives and behind-the-scenes actions. If a person adheres to the principles of truthfulness as a matter of routine, it is easier to relate to them simply because they make it easier for you to understand them and their actions.

If you know that your boss is honest and they claim that a company restructuring is likely in the near future, you can go ahead and believe them point-blank and act accordingly. Instead, if you knew that your boss was a deceptive person, you would most likely scrutinize all their words and actions in as many ways as possible. That is a gigantic waste of time.

Suppose a politician who is reputed for his honesty claims that they will get the locality's roads repaired if they are elected to the municipal election. In that case, you are going to vote for them without thinking about any other aspect. That's the power of honesty within the human mind. And it is because of such force that honesty possesses that we struggle to find public personalities who are totally honest and can be relied upon. It is challenging to maintain honesty over time, especially in cultures that disincentivize it. One of the critical differences between developed countries and the rest of the world is the incentives to honesty in their culture and ethos.

Uncertainty about honesty in a relationship or in a person is mentally debilitating. There are many routine issues of daily life which prove this.

We do not know for sure whether the celebrity endorsing the protein brand actually supports its use or is merely promoting it for financial gain.

We may never know for sure whether the bureaucrat who has held cushy posts throughout their life has actually earned them through competence and hard work or by making tactical compromises.

The romantic college mate of yours may never exactly know for sure whether the diva he is dating is going to ditch him for someone wealthier or fancier than him.

The absence of honesty as an adhesive component in relationships creates a dangerous lack of certainty and balance, which then leads to a lack of emotional and mental security. Sans such security of mind, human endeavours are most likely to remain suboptimal at best. Think about this: With what gusto can you prepare for an exam if you do not really know whether its results are hacked or if you suspect that some candidates may unethically get backdoor access to the question paper by use of money? Would the full faculties of your mind be really dedicated to producing the best output in such circumstances? Most definitely not.

This is why honesty is such a priceless human virtue, which has been extolled for thousands of years. Because it lends balance and security to human lives in a way that most other virtues cannot. And this is precisely why honesty is the primary component of trust in relationships. After all, it is challenging to trust a dishonest person, whatever their other praiseworthy qualities may be.

Another quality that follows naturally from honesty is empathy. In simple language, it means being able to put yourself in someone else's shoes and understand their emotions/viewpoint/concerns. Unless you can truly empathize with someone, you cannot properly relate to their problems or address them. Similar to honesty, empathy is also an innate human characteristic which you develop and possess in your psyche.

If you do not have empathy, you are unlikely to be able to figure out the concerns that your spouse may have about your fidelity in the relationship, and the reasons for such concerns developing over time. An unempathetic partner would most likely dismiss such concerns and never bother to address them. This creates fissures in the relationship, which tend to compound over time and degrade the quality of life for both sides.

A public servant who is not empathetic to the cause of the public and their pressing issues is most likely to spend their time cooped up inside the ivory towers of power. The finer aspects of public life may be completely missing from their mental map, and they only work when they receive a reminder from their superiors, who may in turn have been prompted to act by some major scandal. Such attitudes lead to reactive firefighting, with little thought given to developing better societies. Rampant corruption and a lack of economic development are twin hallmarks of most developing countries, highlighting how the powerful's lack of empathy for the public and society creates substandard conditions for human life.

On a similar note, you also need empathy to thrive in other kinds of relationships. Friendships can quickly turn into exploitation and manipulation if one side recognizes the other's weaknesses and exploits them for personal gain, rather than helping them address the weak spots. Co-workers in the same office may backstab you for the plush foreign assignment and have no compunctions about it. That will make you bitter about professional life, and you will be highly inclined to be on guard at all times.

In short, this is a recipe for the kind of traumatized living that 17th-century English philosopher Thomas Hobbes had conceptualized in his famous Social Contract Theory. Hobbes had postulated how the lack of security can lead to person's life becoming "poor, nasty, brutish and short". Even though Hobbes' ideas were aimed at addressing larger political concerns of society, his understanding remains relevant in the emotional and psychological domains to this day.

Indeed, human lives are often poor, nasty, brutish, and short, and we frequently fight invisible battles within our minds when the security of honesty and empathy is lacking.

8.
People Rarely Change

A painful (and, to an extent, pessimistic) realization that dawns upon "thinking" individuals at some point in time is that you cannot fundamentally "change" people. It has been my understanding that an average human being does not undergo fundamental changes in thinking, attitude and way of life after the hormonal, teenage years. Apart from high-impact, life-changing events, there are very few instruments which can actually "change" a person. Once a person has developed a specific personality, it most certainly remains with them in one form or another.

This fact is something which most of us cannot digest. Across a broad spectrum of society, ranging from hopeless romantics to public servants to social workers, there is a prevailing concept that people can be changed and that their actions can be modified accordingly. However, in reality, "change" in people can be at best an exception and never the norm.

Let us analyze this assessment in the context of the life and work of perhaps the most significant political figure India has produced in contemporary times – Mahatma Gandhi. When we recall Gandhi's life and his principles—truth, Satyagraha, the dignity of labour, etc., we might be tempted to believe that he changed the fabric of Indian society and led India to independence. However, if we dig deeper, did he truly succeed in altering the fundamentals of Indian culture in any way?

After Independence in 1947, India struggled with numerous issues like caste, religion, poverty, corruption, etc. Most of these issues could have been addressed at the societal level had Gandhi's principles actually changed the way people led their lives. Yes, there have been exceptional individuals (like Vinoba Bhave, Lal Bahadur Shastri, Jayprakash Narayan, etc.) who have kept the Gandhian flag flying high. However, such individuals have always been the exception, rather than the norm.

It must be understood here that I do not intend to highlight a God-like figure like Gandhi in a poor light. What I want to convey is that even a towering personality like Gandhi could not fundamentally "change" people. The likes of Ishwarchandra Vidyasagar and Raja Rammohan Roy can be considered in the same light. These were personalities who changed the course of history with their actions and spearheaded social, legal, and cultural renaissance in specific periods, with clear-cut objectives.

Gandhi wanted India to be free from British rule; he worked accordingly. Vidyasagar intended to uplift India's women and acted accordingly. And, they were successful in doing their bit. But, they could never "change" people. They could only create "systems" to achieve what they intended to. Gandhi incorporated his principles into his systematic onslaught against the British. Vidyasagar set up institutions which could survive the test of time and keep the women's cause alive. Raja Rammohan rallied against social evils and set up legal deterrents to protect his commitment and vision.

Despite dedicating their lives to such noble causes, can it be asserted that people today value the dignity of labour or don't commit violence against women or prioritize girls' education? Statistics indicate that violence against women and evils like manual scavenging persist in India. However, the systems (legal, cultural, social) exist, which can be used to tackle these problems. So, if you see your neighbour beating up his wife regularly, you don't need to raise a social movement to protest against it. You can take the help of legal provisions to teach the errant husband a lesson. That's the system that Gandhi, Vidyasagar, Rammohan Roy and other such towering personalities have helped create.

Note how such towering personalities who had the best interests of society at heart could never "change" people, but only create and nourish systems which can tackle problems from time to time. This is exactly what every individual needs to learn in daily living.

Take any environment – be it at home, school, college or office, you can never expect people around you to conform to your thoughts and ways of living. What you can do, instead, is create systems and boundaries in those environments to better serve your goals and objectives.

Changing people is akin to a miracle. Peter Drucker, one of the foremost thinkers of the 20th century, believed, "*It's not that miracles cannot happen. It's just that you cannot depend on them.*" Betting your life on changing people is like depending on a miracle. If a person truly believes in the salience of their change, it will happen. However, outside pressure and influence cannot change anyone.

If you expect your sloppy partner to mend their ways and become serious with their professional life, it will not just magically happen. You can surely try various forms of advice and actions to motivate them to change, but that is the most you can do. Unless they "feel" the need to change, it won't happen.

If you are an upfront and honest person who likes to do their work properly in the office, you cannot expect people around you to be honest as per your expectations. You can set high moral standards for people around you to see, but you cannot goad them into becoming something that they don't personally "feel" attuned with. Instead of getting frustrated with people around you being dishonest, it is more peaceful and practical to maintain your way of work and set clear systems and boundaries with people you have to work with.

If you are part of an unhealthy household, you need not spend a lifetime sulking about your misfortune. Instead, you can create systems by which you can ultimately find a way out of the toxicity. That may include steps such as learning to earn on your own, creating small channels of reliance outside your family, etc.

In short, make it a point to create functional systems that serve your goals, rather than trying to develop new human minds. Good systems help influence the human mind to the best possible extent.

9.

The Importance of Self-Worth

This is a general but fundamentally important principle that applies to most relationships that we create in our lives. Having a firm sense of self-worth makes it easy to navigate all types of relationships – whether with parents, spouse, siblings, children, co-workers, friends, or acquaintances. Being fully aware of what we bring to a relationship makes us a well-rounded human being. Relationships do well when they are between people who are themselves complete and do not need an external agent to "make them feel complete".

There are two elements in this principle.

1. You must have some appreciable content/worth/value within you.
2. You must be well aware of your self-worth and its limitations.

If these two elements align well, a person can develop happy and functional relationships throughout society.

Let us consider the case of Brahmanand, a 12-year-old starry-eyed kid. At home, he finds his parents always insisting on the well-known values of society.

Be honest in your intentions.
Be sincere in your personal life.
Be kind to people.

Be ambitious in your life goals.

However, Brahmanand finds it bemusing when he hears his parents discussing the extraction of an extra parcel of land from their ancestral property without informing the rest of the extended family. Where is the honesty in this, he thinks.

When a neighbour requests that Brahmanand's father let him park his car in their vacant parking spot for a day, his father refuses bluntly. Brahma knows that his father owns an additional parking spot, which mostly remains empty. So, why deny the neighbour's polite request, and that too just for a day? Where is the kindness in this?

Once, Brahmanand wanted to attend a quiz competition with his friends on Diwali day. Brahma loved quizzes and excelled at them. However, since the event was being organized in another part of the town, Brahma had to request his father to take him there by car. His father neither agreed to the idea nor allowed Brahma to explore alternative transportation options. He was forced to stay home and attend a meaningless family function, where his parents and relatives endlessly pretended and dramatized their lives for the entire evening. Where is the concern for ambition, Brahma thought.

Needless to say, Brahmanand had a difficult time reconciling his parents' words and actions. He was too young to interpret the problem. However, as he grew up, he understood that his parents were big-time hypocrites who had no issues with cheating their siblings or pretending to be people they were not. Gradually, he grew distant from both his parents as he learned to interpret the ways of the world. His parents would complain that Brahmanand had not grown up to be a good son, but they never acknowledged their own lack of self-appraisal over the years.

In short, Brahmanand's parents were hollow human beings,

lacking the worth and value they claimed to stand for. Such people may create narratives and impressions to suit their lives in the short term. But, sooner or later, their bluff gets called out.

Not being a good judge of your self-worth can be damaging in other types of relationships as well. Romantic relationships, for example, are replete with cases where either partner's lack of self-worth became the bone of contention in apparently happy relationships.

Varun and Deepshikha have been in a relationship for over two years. Both have their own jobs and stay in the same city. However, Varun constantly feels on edge in the relationship for various reasons. Whenever he tries to communicate this to Deepshikha, things invariably take a sour turn, and verbal fights ensue.

Varun is confused about trying to decipher the reasons behind the sourness in the relationship. He cannot pinpoint the reasons, but feels that something is amiss.

In this case, Varun and Deepshikha are compatible enough to live happily. However, problems have arisen due to Deepshikha's inability to assess her own worth accurately. Deep, as Varun affably nicknames her, has the needless habit of being overly friendly to people. So, despite her hectic professional schedule, she frequently plans get-together events at her place with friends and colleagues. While there is nothing wrong with arranging such events, Deep is not particularly well-versed in the art of managing such events. She always brings Varun in for the preparation and execution of the parties, but rarely bothers to pay heed to Varun's advice on the same. Varun, on his part, tries to do his bit but subconsciously knows that something will always ruin such events.

Sometimes, Deep forgets to pay the water vendor on time, which leads to water issues for subsequent parties.

At other times, Deep invites way too many people to an event, and everybody feels stuck and irritated.

Deep is also overweight. Despite Varun's constant reminders about the need to get in shape, she does not take up any constructive activities for weight loss. Of late, she has become a habitual snorer while sleeping. This makes it difficult for Varun to plan sleepovers at her place. He is a light sleeper and finds it extremely difficult to tolerate such casual behaviour.

Needless to say, Varun has tried to communicate his concerns to Deepshikha on several occasions. However, to no avail, his advice and reminders have been brushed aside. The number of such issues has compounded over time, which has constantly gnawed at the health of the relationship.

This is a clear case of a person damaging a relationship by not understanding their own capabilities or limitations. Having clarity about your own capabilities helps solve such problems in relationships from time to time. Brahmanand's parents could have developed a deeper and more foolproof bond with their son had they recognized the damage that their hypocrisy was creating in their son's mind. They portrayed themselves as people they were not in reality. Similarly, Deepshikha should have realized how her carelessness was ruining what was otherwise a happy relationship.

Clarity of self-worth is thus a core ingredient for forming good relationships. You should know who you are and where your boundaries are drawn. And this should be communicated to the person at the other end of the relationship with no equivocation. As is the case with most of the ideas suggested in the book, such clarity appears to be amazingly simple in principle but equally rare in reality.

Most people struggle in various kinds of relationships due to this fundamental lack of self-awareness.

10.
Good Advice and Bad Advice

The perks of good advice need no validation. We are fully aware of success stories in which mentors played a significant role in the success of their proteges. From Chanakya and Chandragupta Maurya, to Aristotle and Alexander the Great, to Ramakant Achrekar and Sachin Tendulkar, the priceless value of sound advice has come a long way.

However, over-relying on advice can be suicidal. It is this over-reliance on advice which is spelling doom for Indian youth at present. There are too many "advisers" for the youth of today. Starting from their family members to extended family, there is an army of influencers, motivation gurus and lifestyle coaches waiting to grab their attention at every possible opportunity. With so much free advice available, it becomes difficult to ignore it.

The problem is not with advice and counselling as such, but with the agenda and motive behind such advice. I have found that advice is one of the biggest culprits responsible for apparently normal relationships going down the drain.

The chapter on the role of third persons in relationships, which is presented later in the book, will provide a perspective on advice in the context of romantic relationships. For now, let us explore the concept of "coloured" advice through the lens of the student-teacher relationship.

Let us consider the case of young people aspiring to India's premier civil services, for which they must clear a rigorous examination process designed and executed by the Union Public Service Commission (UPSC).

Preparing for the UPSC Civil Service Examination is an industry in itself. Several media reports suggest that this industry is worth approximately Rs 3,000 crores. Having been associated with the UPSC "fraternity" for some time, I have developed a fair understanding of the way advice is dispensed in UPSC preparation circles.

Take the UPSC coaching industry, for example. Most of the "mentors" in this industry appear to be eternally optimistic, bombastically forward-looking, and the veritable personification of "messiah" for the "struggling" UPSC aspirants. Spending 30 minutes with such UPSC coaches and mentors can be life-changing – you might even end up feeling like a superhero who can conquer entire planets. However, such motivation is short-lived. Within a day or two, typical UPSC aspirants return to being what they generally are.

Do I have a problem with such coaches and mentors? Of course NOT.

Do I have a problem with the way they work? Definitely YES.

In the garb of offering free advice and motivation to UPSC aspirants, these advisers are toiling away to keep their own business ventures alive. They either run coaching institutes directly or are associated with one or more of them.

The more motivation they dish out, the more their cult following grows. The more their following, the better the chances of recruiting more aspirants and filling their own coffers. This strategy cannot work well if aspirants start thinking independently and make their own decisions. So, they will motivate the aspirants to keep trying their "luck" for the UPSC exam, with repeated use of ridiculous and theatrical statements like – *Jab tak todenge nahi, tab tak choddenge nahi* (As long as I don't crack it, I won't give up).

The problem is that such advice and motivation are, at a certain level, utterly rubbish. Merely using theatrics and out-of-context motivational language to boost the dopamine levels of under-informed youth is nothing short of misdirection. Aspirants who have failed the exam multiple times are often advised to continue their preparation without exploring other options. Lakhs of such misguided aspirants end up wasting precious years of their career because of such rotten advice.

Advice makes sense when it is offered without a significant agenda. However, in the present times, the morality of providing advice without an agenda is often lost on society. Anybody from your friendly neighbourhood uncle to the crowd at the local tea shop can have an agenda in offering advice.

Some people may be offering advice even without having the relevant credentials. Some people want to push you into a loop of financial extraction. Some people are jealous of what you are and deliberately want to harm you with wrong information. Some people are not worth anyone's time.

In short, it is fair to say that not being alive to the dangers of asking for advice is dangerous. Never seek advice from people without doing background research on the people you are relying on.

Agenda-driven advice can be even more damaging when it is offered by those whom we consider to be safe and credible. Take parents, for example. They are the most credible and trusted source of information for us till we get exposed to others in schools and colleges. Advice offered by parents is taken by children at face value, and the dangers of such advice being selfish and motivated should concern everyone.

Contrary to what society often leads us to believe, not all parents are conscientious and benevolent towards their children. Nor are they the living embodiment of Gods that some want us to believe. Becoming a parent is indeed a life-changing experience for most people, but not everyone changes in the right direction.

Selfish, narcissistic and negative people may not necessarily transform into noble souls by virtue of parenthood. In fact, their problematic traits may only be enhanced and reinforced when they become parents. Some studies show that a narcissistic woman, for example, tends to become more of a narcissist as a mother. She uses her experience of childbearing to extract more physical and psychological privileges from those around her – and this includes the child. Advice offered by such a mother is disproportionately influenced by her own narrow-mindedness rather than logic and reason.

Friends, too, can be damaging when it comes to advice. Some of the most harmful habits, such as smoking and drinking, that we pick up in life can be easily traced back to peer pressure and the influence of charismatic friends. People who are easily swayed by others' opinions and lack clarity in life are highly prone to being exploited and taken advantage of by friends.

This is why I always advise people to differentiate carefully between friends and acquaintances. Most of us are surrounded by acquaintances. We know them because they were with us at the same place at the same time. They will not be with us for long. We need not necessarily judge them as demons, but why should such temporary people have the right to influence our permanent life choices?

Why should you decide on a career which seems the most "in thing" while in college?

Why should you need to waste time looking cool on social

media just because your charismatic co-worker does so?

Why should you become a drinker and smoker just to "belong" to friends' circles when such habits throw our financial and physical health down the drain?

Why should anyone do anything that is damaging to them, just because of advice or influence? It makes no sense. We need to open our senses to logic and rationality as early as possible in life. Learning the art of differentiating what is good or bad for you is one of the most precious lessons that we can acquire early in life. Open your senses, learn to assess advice for its pros and cons, and choose your options for your own betterment. This does not mean you have to become intensely selfish in life. Instead, the emphasis is on negating bad advice and influence, which is generally the output of many relationships in life.

The thumb rule is that advice makes sense when it is offered dispassionately and without any underhanded agenda.

11.
The Nice Person Syndrome

"Nice" is one of the most maligned words in the English dictionary. If one were to go by self-declaration, the world is filled with too many "nice" people. However, reality is different, especially when we start defining what "nice" actually means. Instead of delving too deeply into the realms of psychology and human behaviour, I would prefer to highlight the practical aspects of "niceness" from a layman's perspective. These are not established or universal classifications in any way, but a simple categorization of the various kinds of people around us who claim to be "nice".

The following are the two basic and common types of "nice" people we see around us:

1. **The Doormat:** They are virtually non-existent individuals who exist physically but have no presence in society. They are easy to push over, maintain no long-term principles, try to avoid conflict and confrontation at all costs, and ultimately achieve nothing substantial in life. They are used and abused by various kinds of people in their personal and professional lives. They are like climbers or creepers that grow on whatever support is available. They are not toxic by themselves, but become agents of toxicity when used by the Manipulators. They find it challenging to adhere to even the simplest of principles and struggle to hold to

their word in times of crisis. As consolation, they call themselves "nice" people.

2. The Manipulator: They are extremely affable on the outside and toxic inside. They are experts at lying, cheating and manipulating others. However, their expertise lies in their outward show of friendliness and warmth, which tends to disarm most people. The toxicity they generate will inevitably affect your life. However, because they are outwardly likeable, they will brand themselves "nice" at all times and flaunt that badge around to harm people in various invisible ways, which are difficult to point out. These people are extremely difficult to tackle because their snake-like characteristics make them challenging to spot and tough to hunt.

Let us go through the concept of the Doormat with some examples.

Milind is a diligent student in a top-tier engineering college. He attends classes regularly (which most of his peers don't) and behaves courteously with the professors. He even lends his handwritten notes to his friends before the exams, so that they can secure passing marks without ever attending classes. Since he is not exactly the colloquial "cool dude", he tries to be gentle and modest with girls but can never find the wind to express his "feelings".

Despite his apparent "niceness", defined in terms of courteousness, modesty and helpfulness, Milind is mostly considered a caricature by his friends and other fellow college-mates. He is never sought after in the popular events at his college. Mostly, he is referred to as a "nerd," despite the fact that his hard work is responsible for many students passing their exams. Girls are not interested in him because he lacks the typical alpha-male characteristics. In all, despite being "nice", Milind feels frustrated with his life as a college student.

Or, take Sakshi as a case study. She is one of the most helpful girls in the hostel, and leaves no stone unturned when it comes to helping those in need. She helps her friends with their college assignments, shares her personal room with fellow hostelers in times of need, occasionally cooks food for those who may be ill, and always wears a pleasant smile on her face. Yet, behind her back, her friends mostly call her a "people pleaser". She is viewed as someone who is always "too available". Thus, she is not given the value which she ought to get.

Being "nice" at your workplace can be hazardous, especially in the 21st century.

1. You are dispensable and easily replaceable.
2. Nobody respects you because you can be pushed around.
3. Your co-workers will use you to get their work done, but you may not even have the stomach to ask for simple favours from the same people who took your help.

Workplaces in India are filled with such "nice" people who lose their sense of reality while trying to please everyone. Whether it's the boss, a colleague, or a cook, the archetypal nice person always tries to cosy up to whoever they are interacting with. And because they always want to appear "nice" to people around them, they subconsciously only say things which others want to hear. So, they agree with the boss's observations, who believes that their entire team is useless. They also smile and agree with their colleagues who consider the boss to be a good-for-nothing. In the end, they turn out to be someone with no mind of their own.

Once a person's identity is established on such lines, they are merely a joke to the people around them. Especially in a workplace, such a person is rarely reliable and hence not given essential responsibilities.

When it comes to relationships, it is primarily "nice" partners who end up being betrayed, neglected, cheated upon or hurt. Social media is filled with sob stories of friendly people, yet they lost out in their relationships because of it. What such people often don't realize is that their supposed niceness can have multiple interpretations for their partner in a relationship.

Let us consider the hypothetical case of Rahul and Simran, both of whom are co-workers at an MNC and have been in a relationship for some time. Simran believes herself to be the living personification of the ideal girlfriend and is always "nice" with Rahul.

If Rahul says he has diarrhoea and that he should monitor his food habits, Simran says yes.

If on the same day, Rahul proposes a party with food and alcohol, Simran says yes again.

If Rahul asks her opinion on the suitable venue for a dinner date, Simran says she is happy with whatever Rahul decides.

After all, Simran feels she should agree to whatever Rahul says! Rahul, on the other hand, realizes that his partner does not have a mind of her own and, after some time, decides to break up.

Simran feels that even though she was always "nice" to him, Rahul ditched her for no reason. She goes on to blame God for being cruel to friendly people like her. Instagram and Facebook are filled with such sob stories.

What such friendly people often do not realize is that their niceness can actually become a source of toxicity in their relationships. Becoming a doormat does not necessarily help you hang on to people. Instead, it degrades the overall quality of life.

The Doormats lack a concrete view of reality. They tend to confuse being nice with being courteous/kind. While courtesy and kindness are admirable qualities, being overly friendly can often lead to being a doormat.

If we were to exclude the spiritual world from the discussion, the material world operates on cold, hard logic. Centuries ago, Sigmund Freud observed that the overwhelming majority of people operate according to the basic principle of pain and pleasure. People are incessantly working, both consciously and subconsciously, to reduce their pain and increase their pleasure.

The Doormats do not grasp this concept, and are themselves an exception to the rule. They would willingly accept self-sacrifice and harm to their self-interest, just so that others can "feel" good. They have this twisted view of reality, wherein they believe that by making people around them feel good, they can create better lives, even if it entails their own discomfort.

Besides, the Doormats also lack a sound understanding of human nature. They suffer from delusions of reciprocation. They tend to assume that, with their behaviour, which is often perceived as spineless by the outside world, they can "earn" the niceness of the people they interact with/live with.

So, the nice man may assume that by being overly polite with a co-worker, who is actually cunning and corrupt, they can actually get that person to behave politely with him.

Or, the nice lady may assume that she should let her husband keep beating her up every night just so that her submission might persuade the husband to behave differently someday.

In neither of these two situations do the Doormats realize the fundamental flaw in their assumptions, the element of human nature. While human beings are touted to be the most evolved creatures on Earth, they are extremely difficult to "change" once their baseline personality has been formed.

So, a boy who grows up to become a wife-beater is unlikely to transform into a saint because the wife behaves like a doormat.

And a corrupt employee shall continue to be corrupt, irrespective of how "nicely" his co-worker behaves with him.

Sometimes, being overly friendly can also be a sign of spinelessness. If you don't have a backbone, you can never take a principled stand on any issue in life. If your in-laws consistently berate you in the presence of your spouse, and your spouse does not object to it, it simply means that your spouse is spineless. There may be euphemisms used to justify such cowardly behaviour, but it does not change the truth.

They may come up with excuses like:

Let's keep things peaceful. Conflict within a family is not healthy.

Let's not be disrespectful. Elders know better.

However, there is no denying that they lack the courage to take a stand on an issue that deserves their intervention. Such spinelessness is directly attributable to the fact that some people are mentally wired to be subservient. It is very easy to boss over them, because they rarely fight back and are always trying to "maintain peace". If you ever encounter such a person, always remember that they are incapable of making decisions for themselves. If you rely on them in any way, they are incapable of standing up for you.

The Manipulators are actually the real winners when it comes to "nice" people. This is because they can effectively combine persuasive real-life acting skills with a solid understanding of human nature.

The "nice" colleague at your office, whom you have worked with for more than three years, secretly hates your technical competence, which earns you the boss's attention and praise. They know that if things go well, you are likely to get promoted and even get rewarded with a foreign assignment within a year. They are jealous of your success, but will craftily hide their real emotions and remain in everyone's good books. You share many of your household stories with them, some of which are pretty sensitive. Because they are charming and apparently "nice", you feel at ease in sharing these stories with them. On one occasion, you shared with them an instance when you went through a rough patch in your marriage and had regular arguments with your spouse at home.

The nice colleague also has access to the boss, who knows that you are far superior to them in competence and skills. However, nice colleague has silently started the campaign of poisoning the boss's mind about you to scuttle your progress. Not so surprisingly, you don't have a whiff about such a thing happening. Even the boss does not precisely know why the nice colleague is making certain "soft" statements regarding you. They are so subtle that even if anyone were to record all their verbal and written communication with you or the boss, they would not be able to discern their real agenda. Their niceness helps keep people around them fuzzy.

Finally, after a year or so, when you are expecting to hear the good news of promotion and foreign travel, you hear that nice colleague has been selected in your place. They are so lovely that they give you the news themselves, making it appear as if the boss was unjust with you and gave them the assignment, which they did not really want! Since their niceness knows no bounds, they even help you understand how bosses exploit employees with the lure of rewards which never come. You are confused and dejected, but feel at ease with nice colleague, who has been so nice to you even in such distress.

This is nothing but a scam. The Manipulators can pull off such scams with such expertise that they are challenging to track down and hold accountable. In the above example, would you really bother having confidential meetings with your boss, or would your boss bother to have a clear word with you after nice colleague's psychological adventures? Most likely not, unless the relationship between you and your boss is secured by a high degree of trust.

In romantic relationships as well as marriages, such scamsters are all around us. They will win our trust with their charming and affable personalities, and then harm us in ways we may not even fully understand. Sometimes, breakups happen, and the cheating partner parts ways, saying the loyal one is to blame for not being able to hold them properly in the relationship.

The real problem in tackling such Manipulators is their niceness. Outwardly, they are so lovely that nobody has the appetite to investigate their behaviour and expose them for what they are. In fact, exposing them in itself makes you a "bad" person unless you can literally nail them with evidence or catch them red-handed, which becomes close to impossible when it comes to psychological manoeuvres and emotional issues.

Manipulators can be handled only using their own medicine. They can never be cured, but your boundaries and behaviour can signal to them that you are not someone to mess with. This should not be done through direct one-on-one confrontations. Neither does this mean that you have to transform yourself into a villain to confront another villain. It is all about engaging in what I like to call "*emotional warfare*". This kind of warfare is undertaken when you know that you are fair, kind and harmless to people around you, and yet you are taken advantage of by those who like to prey upon good souls like you.

A detailed discussion of this form of warfare is beyond the scope of this book. However, it mostly conforms to the rules of Defensive Realism, which is a well-known theory in international relations. Broadly, it suggests that one should be aware of the practical aspects of human nature, which encompasses both positive and negative elements, and be prepared to defend oneself at all times. The assumption is that you may be attacked by elements who pander to the harmful aspects of human nature, and hence you need to protect yourself by various means. Aggression is one of the means of protection which should be used to scare off the attacker when underhand tactics do not show results. Mind and word games should be in your arsenal as well. In short, the attacker should "know" that trying to harm you is not beneficial to them. This concept has parallels with the idea of Dharma in Hindu philosophy, which has been popularized across the ages by Shri Krishna's sermons to Arjuna in the Mahabharata war, as recorded in the *Bhagavad Gita*.

Now comes the moot question: How to tackle life in general and relationships in particular when you are clear about not becoming a Doormat or a Manipulator to be vaguely nice? I have some practical prescriptions here.

1. Becoming "purposeful" by embracing "Enlightened selfishness": It is my understanding that selfishness is too harshly treated, highly misinterpreted, and vilified in today's world. Our society would transform dramatically if only people stopped the hypocrisy surrounding selfishness and started embracing "enlightened selfishness". A person as renowned as Mahatma Gandhi had endorsed the concept of enlightened self-interest. In layperson's terms, it simply means that a person deserves to keep themselves at the centre of their own world. But at the same time, he also accepts the fact that others are also allowed to do the same. This helps create self-sufficient individuals who are neither interested in exploiting others nor willing to accept being exploited by others. This prescription makes sense because it acts like a general disclaimer, if I know that both you and I are going to protect our fair interests in the long run, we are unlikely to waste each other's time by trying to exploit or be exploited. Problems occur when one side senses and exploits the weaknesses in the other side to its own benefit. People who are obsessed with being nice find it challenging to term themselves selfish.

2. **Observation + Reality + Facts:** I like to call this the ORF Formula. You should learn to observe well, which in itself is a difficult skill to master with time. Most people love to live senselessly because it is easy, and you can go with the flow. Observation requires patience and the application of one's mind. If you learn the skill to observe people and society, you are most likely to discover the many predictable elements in them. When you become a good reader of life and living, you become a good judge of situations and circumstances. This is possible when you actually use your senses to soak in "reality" and "facts" and not linger on vague concepts of life. What does not make sense will start dawning on you; you will be able to decode the ways of the manipulative co-worker or the untrustworthy partner and what they mean. This will help you see through "transactions" for what they are and decipher the "currency" with which you are dealing – it can be money, emotions, trust, or something else. A person receiving extra attention all of a sudden, or an employee being praised by the boss for unusual reasons, or a friend ghosting you after taking liberal loans and never repaying them, are such transactions in relationships which need to be understood in real terms.

3. **The Art of Saying NO:** This is the most powerful lesson that any person can learn, internalize and execute in life. If used properly, the power to say "NO" can have a transformative impact on the lives of individuals. The real problem with nice people, and especially the Doormats, is that they rarely learn the art of saying "no" in their lives. Saying NO should come from a standpoint of principle and logic, so that it becomes easy. If you know that

weekend parties are a waste of both time and money, you can say NO without much thinking and without even considering fuzzy questions like, "What would my friends think if I did not attend the party?" or "Would I be called names if I do not go to parties?"

There is no glory in being exploited. Covertly exploiting others, psychologically and emotionally, is an act of cowardice of the highest order. There is nothing nice about either of them. Accept that and move on with better aspirations for life.

12.
The Excitement Trap

Twenty-first-century life is supposed to be "cool" and "happening". At least, that is what society (nowadays reflected on social media) wants us to believe. So, if you happen to be a youngster without anything "cool" going on in your life, you may feel left out. I have already mentioned this in the context of finding the ideal romantic partner in one of the earlier chapters.

Being cool/exciting/happening usually means a lot of things in the common lingo:

1. Cursing your regular office job, even though you may not really be good enough to do anything else.
2. Travelling across the world, even though you have no clue where your savings are going to be replenished from.
3. Drinking, clubbing, partying and whatnot so as to feel the "buzz", even though you may not exactly have the taste buds for alcohol or the appetite for meaningless parties.
4. Going solo, which means not getting married and instead having multiple short-lived relationships, which are easy to create and extinguish.

The list is not exhaustive, and you will definitely come across numerous other things which can be included in the definitions. This fad of being cool usually runs its course by the time people get into their 30s and reality kicks in. However, too many people make a mess of their 20s in the quest to be cool and happening.

The reality, however, is not exactly "cool". Life is boring and unexciting for most parts. Let's investigate the four propositions of excitement I pointed out earlier a bit more closely.

1. Those hating their boring, regular jobs may end up hopping on too many ships in the quest for excitement and end up nowhere. Disliking your job is perfectly fine, but the way you look for alternatives should make sense and not be based merely on "excitement quotient". Without qualities like discipline, professionalism and integrity, you are unlikely to survive and thrive in any job, however exciting it may initially be.
2. You have a colleague who loves travelling and takes expensive foreign trips with his wife twice every year. This creates the itch of excitement within you. However, you are not aware of the fact that this colleague was fortunate enough to be born and married into rich families. You may very well love travelling, but without meticulous financial planning, you might end up bankrupt very soon if you try to follow this colleague for the sake of excitement. There are too many stories of professionals going into debt despite their fat pay cheques.
3. Being a "party animal" or alcoholic is not necessarily the only way to feel included in 21st-century social groups. Neither partying nor consuming alcohol are to be looked down upon, but making them the criteria for a person's acceptability in social circles is complete rubbish. There are too many young professionals today who are forced to become alcoholics and "party-lovers" because they would otherwise feel left out and stigmatized. In short, there is no God-given decree that Friday

and Saturday nights are to be mandatorily spent in bars and pubs. You might as well spend them sleeping, cuddling your dog or reading.

4. While getting into relationships is one kind of fad, the other end of the spectrum has people not committing to marriages just for the sake of appearing fashionable. There are people who are predetermined about not marrying because of various flimsy reasons. Marrying or not marrying is a personal decision, but it ought to be taken because of personal preferences and long-term values, and not the trends around us. By the time you are in your mid-30s, and no longer surrounded by fashionable, cool people, a severe hollowness might creep in. This is extremely dangerous and may lead to several physical and mental ailments.

The key point I am trying to make is that whatever you do should be based on sound logic and reasoned principles that make sense to you, and not on the fashion of the time.

If you decide to remain unmarried, then that's your choice. But when you feel lonely later on, you should be able to defend your own decision to yourself.

If you hate your job and desperately want to get out of it, then have your own tailor-made plans.

If you love alcohol, then drink to your heart's content if you can afford it. Just know that when it takes a toll on your health, you are ready to blame your own habits.

When it comes to relationships, it is again prevalent thinking that "being with someone" is supposed to be exciting. It is believed to give you the "feel-good" vibes at all times. This is not true. Having a partner is all about creating a system of living in which you share your life with someone else, who, in return, shares their life with you. It is definitely not "exciting" in colloquial terms once the initial euphoria has worn off.

People getting into relationships for the sake of excitement and fun are inevitably disappointed once routine sets in. Even the most handsome man or beautiful woman can seem boring after living with them daily for years. Such excitement-seekers often turn out to be serial cheaters in relationships and are seldom trustworthy with precious emotions and life's most essential elements.

Relationships, much like mutual fund investments, should be viewed from a long-term perspective. Those investing in the stock market in the hope of quick gains are frequently disappointed. Similarly, some people enter into relationships for the rush of adrenaline or to fill their time. Wise people know that you have to invest in the right relationship for long periods of time, in a boring yet systematic manner, to reap the rich rewards in the long term. If you find someone who is dull, unexciting, and yet potentially good for a long-term commitment, go right ahead with such a person.

When it comes to life and living, the most successful people have often been the most boring and unexciting ones. They have preferred routine and monotony for their entire lives to achieve success. Be it Warren Buffett, Mahatma Gandhi, or Roger Federer. you read the story of any successful person and you will find the mention of how they have stuck to monotonous routines over long periods of time. Mark Manson, in his quirky book *The Subtle Art of Not Giving a F*ck*, has shown that most human beings have to put up with various hardships and problems in life; and what we should be concerned about is not that life needs to be stress-free and lovely, but that we sign up for the right kind of hardships in life. Thus, it is better to struggle to be a successful lawyer than to be a thief and struggle to flee from prison.

The same principle applies to success in relationships as well. Monotony and lack of excitement shall be an inevitable reality in any relationship you get into.

Best friends who chat for hours may not talk for more than five minutes every six months, as the years roll on.

Even the most physically attractive person does not evoke much excitement in us if we share the same space with them for a specific period of time.

What really matters is whether we chose the right relationships to persevere with. Whether the person at the other end of the relationship really fits into our world seamlessly and progressively makes it better. As we mature in a relationship, the intangible aspects, love, trust, commitment, and value systems, should be prioritized over the tangible elements. Only on the back of such intangible assets of the relationship can it be persevered with.

On a humorous note, the importance of long-term stability in relationships is nowhere more evident than in matrimonial advertisements, where those with boring yet stable government jobs tend to hog the limelight!

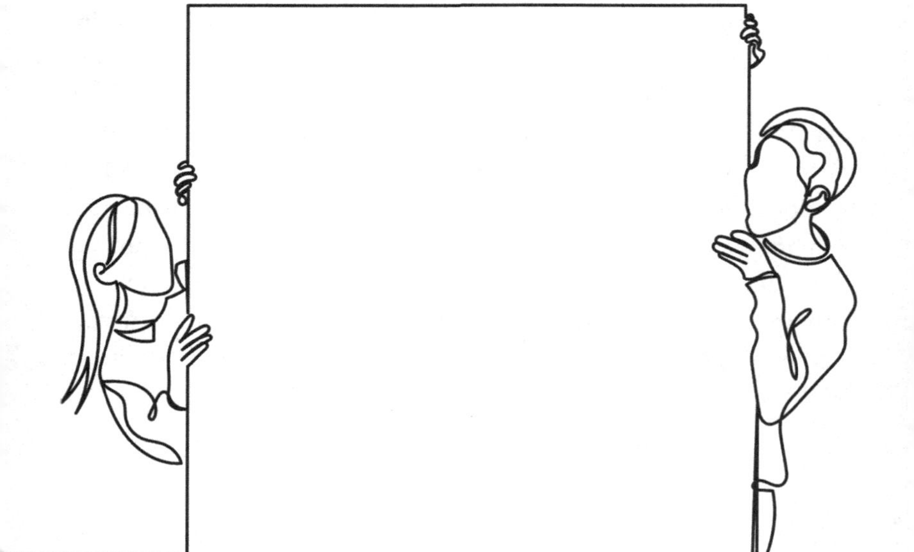

13.
Behind the Scenes

Psychology, even in its most basic and rudimentary form, has a massive role to play in everyone's life. However, most of us hardly ever bother with psychology, given that studying the subject academically does not yield astronomical pay packages anywhere. Those who might actually study the subject academically may not be fully aware of its practical implications.

Survival in society relies strongly on psychology and patterns in human thinking and behaviour. The way you think decides the way you act. And the way you behave determines the consequences you face. Depending on the consequences you face, you start thinking and acting again. This works in a cycle.

The biggest weakness that I have noticed in youngsters is their reluctance to learn the art of thinking. I am not referring to the content of "what" you think. Instead, I am more concerned about "how" you think. If the how is understood and assimilated over time, the "what", "when", and "why" become easier to tackle.

Let's take a very common example: Young people getting hurt/cheated/bluffed in their relationships. Bollywood has been kind enough to teach an entire generation of Indian youth that life makes no sense if you don't have a partner in your teens/20s. In fact, those who survive without a girlfriend or boyfriend are often labelled as losers.

To escape such a fate, most youngsters make their best efforts to pair up as soon as possible. Needless to say, most of these pairs from their teenage or early 20s wither away very soon. This leaves either the boy or the girl badly scarred, psychologically. It is for this psychologically hurt segment of the youth that I wish to point out the basics of "thinking".

Most human beings, at least till their early 30s, operate on binary terms, pain and pleasure. They seek to minimize their pain and maximize their pleasure. Greatest philosophers, such as Sigmund Freud and Jeremy Bentham, have pointed out that most human beings operate on the pain-pleasure principle throughout their lives. Although it is unfair to generalize that the entire human civilisation operates on this principle at all times, it is indeed true for many people for substantial periods. So, whenever you share any part of your life with a person, try to understand their pain and pleasure points.

Let's say your girlfriend ditched you all of a sudden. In such a situation, you don't need to feel instantly blank or hopeless. Instead, you should be practical enough to understand that the girl's potential pleasure in ditching you possibly outweighs the pain in staying with you. Sometimes, you may not be at fault. But the other side may see more pleasure in doing something else, which may betray your expectations. Having such clarity of mind and thinking in such pinpointed terms keeps you stable when you get into a mess of relationships where your life is affected by other people's behaviour, and you may have done nothing particularly wrong to them.

That is why I always advise people to never waste time on those who lack higher thinking capabilities and tend to operate on the pain-pleasure principle obsessively. Such people, after a certain age, are never respected. For example, if you spot a friend who is sharing someone else's secrets with you regularly, you can be pretty sure that they are doing the same with your secrets. They derive pleasure from such an exchange of information with others, and it may have nothing to do with more honourable and higher-order concepts such as integrity and commitment.

If you can learn the ability to spot the pain and pleasure points of people you deal with, you will go way ahead of the rest of society in terms of thinking capabilities. Let's see some of the most common pleasure points for people:

1. Money
2. Sympathy/Care
3. Attention
4. Fame

There can be many such pleasure points for different people, which you will discover along the way. If your girlfriend cheated on you for no apparent fault of yours, it might be so that someone else offered her greater pleasure on some aspect which she values, maybe sympathy, attention or money. When it comes to issues such as power and authority, it is often money that proves to be the primary motivator for those in power. This also tends to be the source of corruption.

However, all this does not mean that you turn yourself into a loner to avoid such people who are driven by the pain-pleasure principle. It simply means that you are aware of their existence and would know how to handle them. In fact, at any given time in life, you will mostly deal with people who have clear agendas for pleasure. They may "say" and "act" in ways which are suggestive of their nobility of character, but with some astute and patient observation, you must be able to figure out what the person "really wants".

So, if you earn a job and get backstabbed by an extremely

friendly colleague, you should know how to think about the situation. Instead of feeling low and consigning your situation to destiny, see through the reasons why that fellow harmed you. With minimal scrutiny, you may find out the reason, they wanted the corner office!

Even though the pain-pleasure principle might drive the overwhelming majority of people, it is worthwhile to mention that the world remembers and honours those who grew past its temptations and lived for higher causes. India's freedom fighters will be remembered for centuries because they had evolved beyond the pain-pleasure principle and dedicated their lives to a sacred cause. The British may have never left India if they could have lured all prominent Indians with money and fame.

There is life beyond this principle. But human society is still evolving, and it will take time before we reach such levels of collective thinking that living for a nobler cause becomes second nature. Daniel Pink, in his best-selling book *Drive*, has highlighted the changing nature of motivation in human beings based on the growth and evolution of societies.

India's start-up culture is a silver lining that can be analyzed in this context. Start-ups cannot survive and flourish if the founders are merely driven by pleasure and repulsed by pain. Similarly, a mature human relationship is also a cause, which involves both partners going above their basal pleasures to do justice to the relationship code.

Whatever you are and wherever you are, always design your life around a cause higher than yourself. It may be religious, political, social, technological, etc. Without a higher cause, human evolution is quite incomplete.

14.
Words, Actions, and Events

Getting into a romantic relationship is exciting. Persisting in one and being reasonably happy, though, is much tougher. By virtue of several factors, both within and outside the relationship, most relationships tend to get progressively complicated over time. Some are so confusing that people in them waste years wondering whether to stay or break it off.

It is such confusion and fuzziness of the mind that takes a toll on our happiness and mental health. A relationship that we once considered the source of ecstasy and fulfilment may soon turn into an abyss of dreaded confusion and misinterpretations.

It is thus essential to maintain a clear understanding of a relationship's health periodically. While social media is abuzz with terms like "red flag" and "green flag", I shall refrain from such cliché terms in this chapter. Instead, I advise people to set milestones in any relationship they enter. Such milestones should be interspersed with markers which indicate whether the relationship is on the correct track.

In this context, the importance of words, actions, and events is to be interpreted.

Words: If a relationship were like a bottle, words would fill more than 80 per cent of the space in it. They constitute the fundamental element of any relationship between two human beings. In fact, language is one of the foremost determinants of human civilisation, and sets it apart from other animals. Without words and language (verbal and non-verbal), it isn't easy to sustain any relationship.

Actions: This is the second layer of connection, which makes any relationship "worth it". Words should ideally translate into appropriate actions. This signals the sound health of a relationship. However, it is unrealistic to think that words translate into actions in all relationships without much ado. In fact, most relationships tend to break down when words are present but appropriate actions are absent.

Events: These are the milestones in any relationship. Words and actions are the markers along the way. Events signal that the relationship has reached a certain point and should potentially progress well. However, merely organizing events without going through the established markers can be disastrous. Simply having a grand marriage ceremony followed by lavish birthday parties and anniversary nights cannot sustain a relationship.

The thumb rule that I find acceptable and workable, in terms of the importance of these three terms, is: Events > Actions > Words, when the three are followed in chronological order. That means words are less critical than actions, and actions are less important than events when none of the three are skipped. Let us take an example to understand this.

Band and Baaja are in a romantic relationship. Band professes his love to Baaja daily and puts up excellent displays of affection on social media and at friends' gatherings. However, Baaja often finds Band flirting with other girls in the neighbourhood. He even texts some of them regularly when he thinks Baaja is not paying attention to him. When confronted about such behaviour by Baaja, Band dismisses the allegations without having the appetite to go through a rigorous discussion. In this situation, Band's words are present, but his commensurate actions are missing. If Band and Baaja decide to get married (event), problems are likely to compound over time, which will only deteriorate the relationship.

Raavana and Mandakini have recently come through an arranged marriage ceremony. They had a minimal courtship period during which both parties were mainly trying to impress each other using colourful facades. Everything seemed incredible in the short term, until the colour of the facades started fading. Raavana was not happy with Mandakini's sleeping habits – she was a habitual snorer with little care for Raavana's concern. Mandakini hated the fact that Raavana was rarely expressive of love and affection. Raavana neither promised date nights nor weekend getaways, and he never agreed to Mandakini's proposals for the same. The relationship became a nightmare, and both parties suffered. This was a case where the event was formalized in a hurry, but the words and actions necessary to nurture a relationship were left unattended.

Indrajit and Sulochana have been in a long-term relationship in which both parties seem to understand each other quite well. Indrajit is a man of his word and Sulochana understands that she should complement Indrajit's good qualities wherever possible. Their communication is based not just on spoken words but also on unspoken body language. If Sulochana is upset about something and Indrajit senses it, he changes his actions for the day to placate Sulochana without ever telling her that he knows. Sulochana does the same when it comes to Indrajit's life. She complements his ambitions with her actions wherever possible and never seeks credit for the same. Both get married, have kids and get along quite well. Words (spoken and unspoken) were translated into actions, which led to events.

In reality, we rarely encounter such extreme relationships that are either completely bust or always flourishing. Most relationships function at some point in the spectrum between the extremes. There are good and bad phases, but both parties in the relationship need to acknowledge this and work towards aligning their words, actions, and events properly. When things start going lopsided, it becomes a natural responsibility of either partner to take up the challenge and rectify the situation.

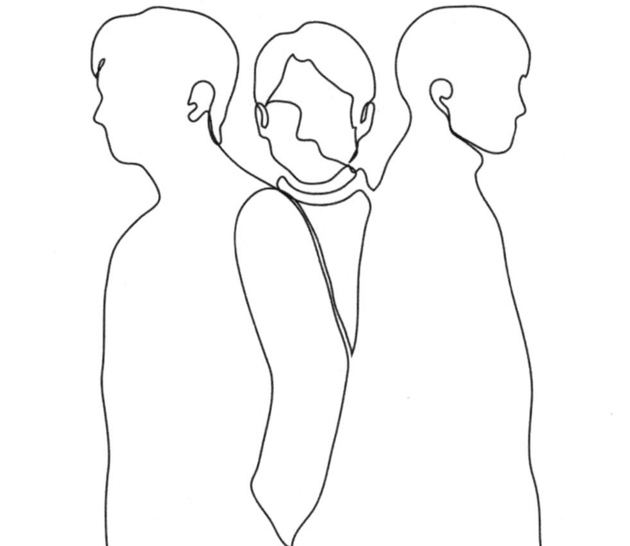

15.
The Third Person

This principle of not letting a third person enter a relationship of two people is of utmost importance in romantic relationships and marriage, in particular. If I were asked about the top three keys to a good relationship, this would be one. A relationship is fundamentally between two people, who are supposed to build it with their own dynamics. The cardinal mistake that most people tend to make in relationships is that they expose these dynamics to outsiders or "third persons". An outsider can be anyone, parents, siblings, friends, co-workers, neighbours, etc.

In the initial phases of a relationship, the partners are generally on cloud nine. The attraction factors are so strong that even the small bumps in the connection are swept away. The bond is tight enough to keep outsiders out of its purview. However, the scenario changes slowly as the initial burst of romanticism fades and unresolved issues begin to accumulate.

Ravi and Vidya were the perfect couple while dating each other. They seemed to be spot on with their mutual understanding. The chemistry was so strong that they hardly bothered to share details of their relationship, even with parents and close friends. Soon, they got married, and the dynamics began to change.

Once parents, friends, and extended family members started learning about their relationship, comments and unsolicited advice occasionally reached both partners. Generally, both Ravi and Vidya tried to ignore such inputs. But during periods of stress, anxiety and misunderstanding, they could no longer avoid such comments and inputs.

Ravi's parents had always warned him about Vidya being too expressive towards outsiders. Ravi had ignored such warnings until the day he fought with Vidya because she appeared to be flirting with a younger man named Alok in the neighbourhood. The inability to resolve the issue between themselves led Ravi to ponder his parents' warning.

Vidya too was carrying her own baggage of feedback, opinions and comments on the relationship. Her best friend, Shreya, had a hunch that Ravi would be a difficult person to put up with because of his over-cautious nature. The fight with Ravi over the issue of flirting with Alok made Vidya think about how accurate Shreya's projection had been. After all, she was merely having a casual conversation with Alok. Why would Ravi act so tough over such a trivial issue?

In any normal relationship, especially in marriage, there will be a host of issues that require patience on both sides to resolve. However, people tend to expose the facts and details of their relationships in times of stress, in the vain hope of getting solace and support. Both Ravi and Vidya, instead of brooding on the comments of people outside the relationship, should have sorted things out between themselves in the clearest possible way.

However, when third parties get details of a relationship, they often chime in with their own perspectives, which may not be particularly relevant to the relationship. In the above example, Shreya's impression of Ravi being over-cautious and hence difficult is based on her own experience with a suspicious boyfriend. Ravi has no connection to that fellow. Yet, Shreya's projection of her life on Ravi and Vidya's relationship is taken seriously because she appears to be a "concerned third party".

Such comments appear accurate in moments of stress because either partner is unable to let go of their ego when confronted with contentious issues. As more such issues remain unresolved and partners silently draw feedback from outsiders, the relationship suffers.

Sometimes, friends and relatives who nurse grudges against you insert their toxic advice into your relationships by appearing extremely benevolent. We always find such people around us who are wolves in sheep's skin. Such people are vengeful by nature, and they make their presence felt whenever we are in distress.

You may be friends with someone who is silently harbouring extreme jealousy towards your personal and professional success, but pretends to be a wiser person. Such a friend can insidiously damage your marriage by offering you sugar-coated, toxic advice from time to time. Their real impact is understood long after the damage is already done.

You may have a narcissistic parent who hates your independent lifestyle, which you have developed from an early age. Such a parent will give you a list of negative things that may happen to you if you make decisions on your own and without grovelling at their feet. They will keep you on the edge at all times. Whenever anything bad happens to you, they will be prompt to point out how accurate their predictions were. Such covertly narcissistic parents desperately want their children to be dependent on them without offering them emotional support in return.

It is therefore essential to establish clear boundaries with outsiders regarding your relationships. It can be parents, siblings, friends, neighbours, or co-workers, but they are all outsiders to the relationship between the two people. The dynamics of the bond are unique and forged between two people based on their own intuition and thinking process. While sensible people generally refrain from making loose remarks in personal matters, the majority of outsiders find such gossip to be very spicy.

Couples should have clarity between themselves regarding the extent to which they shall share details of the relationship with outsiders. This agreement must not be violated, even in moments of stress and confusion. Neither side should discuss thorny issues of the relationship with outsiders, unless such an outsider is a professional who has no vested interest in it.

Maintaining boundaries with third parties ensures that cracks in the relationship are not enlarged over time by outside influences. Most people have little to invest in other people's lives except gossip and chit-chat. Such gossipy advice should not be able to damage relationships which are painstakingly built over time.

16.
Immaturity

Immature people can be broadly categorized into the "Doormats" group of "nice persons," which we analyzed in one of the earlier chapters. Given their significant impact on human relationships, they deserve a separate chapter for detailed analysis and understanding.

Maturity is not something we often actively seek in others. In fact, it is taken for granted that adults around us are mature. With this assumption in mind, we tend to seek out relationships with like-minded adults. Unfortunately, maturity is a precious gift that not everyone possesses. While it may not be considered a quality in itself, maturity is like an adhesive which keeps a person intact during the multifaceted journey of life. It is like air, we need it to survive, but it is always invisible.

One of the major stumbling blocks in modern relationships is a lack of maturity. While the outward expressions and behaviour of a person may show nothing wrong, their maturity in handling relationships is often found wanting. Handling human relationships is an art, and you need a basic level of maturity to excel in this area. That is why managers are paid so highly across organizations because they are supposed to have the maturity to handle complex teams dealing with complex tasks.

Personal relationships are no different either. If either partner lacks the mental and psychological maturity necessary for a healthy relationship, complications are likely to arise from unexpected areas.

Families, for example, are the most common source of problems in romantic relationships, especially in marriages. Let us understand the importance of maturity in relationships by examining the marriage template.

Even though nuclear families are in vogue, the influence of immediate and extended family members on either the husband or the wife is always present. And it makes sense, too. Neither a boy nor a girl can magically become mentally untangled from the people with whom they have been associated for such a long time. With nuclear families becoming the prevalent norm of the day, we mostly see couples becoming physically independent from their families but psychologically connected to them in various invisible ways.

This is where maturity becomes crucial in sustaining a marriage and navigating the challenges and pressures of family life. Let's see why.

Shruti and Vikram are newlyweds after two years of romance. They live away from their parents, in a different city altogether.

Shruti's parents hate loud music or rambunctious sports events on television at home. Shruti is accustomed to growing up in a home where such things are avoided. And, despite her long relationship with Vikram before marriage, she has no idea of how it actually "feels" to be in a home where her husband absolutely loves to be expressive when his favourite sports event comes on TV.

The girl feels a bit lost seeing the difference in ways of living. However, without being judgemental, she occasionally conveys her day-to-day life after marriage to her mother. The mother, unless she is conscious of the fine print of the relationship, may casually express how difficult it must be for her daughter to adjust to her husband's household.

In this case, if Shruti is not mature enough, her mother's casual expressions about the cultural differences between Shruti's parental home and her husband's home may start creating impressions in her mind.

If she starts repeating such points of difference in her mind and adds them to her mother's casual observations, she may soon begin to "feel" unnerved in the marriage. Over time, she will start approaching issues in the wrong way.

Shruti may have frequent fights with Vikram if the issue of sports events on television is not sorted out.

Shruti may find Vikram's financial indiscipline difficult to handle after having seen her father be so meticulous about his family's finances.

Shruti may find Vikram's late-night gaming habits difficult to condone.

If she is unable to work out the problem with her husband, she may start feeling lost very soon. In fact, this is what "real" marriages look like. Once two human beings begin sharing the same physical and mental space, a laundry list of issues will arise. Most of these issues can be resolved with an open mind and a willingness to find a middle ground. However, this is the maturity that is found wanting in most people.

Immature people find it difficult to prosper in relationships because they are unable to grasp the basics. A relationship can exist only when it is "mutually" beneficial. Both sides must feel the benefits of the relationship, and be willing to concede ground on thorny issues.

Another aspect where maturity is most needed is loyalty. If, for some reason, trust issues arise between a couple, a strain of varying degrees can affect the relationship. In such a situation, the most necessary quality on either side is maturity.

If Shruti finds Vikram frequently texting his ex-girlfriend, she will struggle to dismiss her suspicions. She has to communicate her concerns to Vikram and expect an amicable resolution. Vikram, on the other hand, cannot absolve himself of guilt with hollow promises. He needs to demonstrate the maturity to address Shruti's concerns if he genuinely wants the relationship to proceed.

Vikram must be mature enough to work overtime to rebuild the trust that has been broken. This may mean Vikram keeps his cellphone accessible to Shruti at all times and provides answers and accountability to his wife whenever she needs it. If he lacks the sense and maturity to work hard under these circumstances, he will only inject more confusion into the relationship over time.

Not everyone is a born thinker or an expert at handling relationships. However, it is the willingness and honest intent to mentally and emotionally invest in a relationship that drives up the maturity factor in people.

If you build a relationship, it is advisable to invest the necessary energy in learning and improving.

17.
Relationship With Your Boss

Sooner or later, most of you will have a job. Even though the nature of the job may be different for each one of us, a particular aspect shall remain the same across all of them – the Boss!

While a great deal has been written and spoken about the intricacies of our professional lives, the "boss factor" does not receive the kind of attention it deserves. The reality is that a sizeable chunk of the successes and failures that you witness in your professional life is because of your boss.

Bosses are so pivotal to a person's scheme of things that their thoughts and actions tend to have a tremendous impact on the lives of those working under them. Sometimes, bosses are even directly responsible for divorces and deaths among their employees. Certain cold and hard facts about "bosses" must be learnt as early as possible in professional life.

1. Study your bosses thoroughly. Your boss is also a human being driven by interests. Most of us have a very vague understanding of those who supervise us. We often assume that our bosses are more mature and mentally stronger than we are; however, in most cases, that is not true. Your boss will be another human being struggling with their own issues. Outside their office, nobody gives them the seniority that their subordinates do.

So, if the boss is divorced, and you have a thriving family life, it is best not to discuss family issues in front of your boss. They may even maintain a happy face and wish you all the best, but internally, they might be seething with envy as they see your family life flourish. There may be exceptions to this rule, but caution is warranted.

Alternatively, it may be that your boss is a non-performer, and you are drawing the attention of the entire office with your stellar knowledge and performance. In such a situation, most average bosses will do everything in their power to clip the wings of the high-performing subordinate. And, most bosses that you will have are going to be average ones.

It is essential to thoroughly study your boss before determining the best ways to interact with and manage them. Here are some of the typical boss types which you may encounter in your professional life:

(a) **Jealous and Non-Performing:** These bosses rarely get appreciated for their own work and cannot tolerate any of their subordinates being praised for their calibre.

(b) **Mid-Life Crisis:** They have poor or non-functional family lives, which keeps them in a state of constant stress and frustration. They often harbour secret issues with those who lead everyday family lives.

(c) **Indecisive:** They can never make decisions on their own. They force their subordinates to make decisions on their behalf, but will only take credit if the decision turns out to be a good one. For the bad choices, they will vanish.

(d) **Dividing to Rule:** They are ambitious individuals who strive to advance in their own careers. They employ a divide-and-rule policy with their subordinates to ensure complete control.

(e) **Corrupt:** These individuals enter their professional lives with an active predisposition to corruption. Such individuals tend to flourish for some time, provided they possess other qualities, such as diligence and technical expertise. However, sooner or later, they are burned by their own karma.

There are many such varieties of bosses, and some may even offer exciting combinations of these types. It is essential to study and identify the kind of person you are dealing with.

2. Do not turn your boss into a parent: There is a prevailing misconception that your office is supposed to be akin to your family. Nothing could be further from the truth and more hazardous to mental health. The most dangerous thing is to consider your office to be another family and the boss to be a family member.

As I have already pointed out, hardly 1 out of 100 bosses you find in real life will be exceptional. The remaining 99 will be average human beings. Most youngsters, early on in their professional careers, tend to have unrealistic expectations of their bosses. They tend to consider their bosses to be their mentors, guides, philosophers, and so on. This is unhealthy and problematic in many ways.

Turning your boss into a parent/mentor/guide involves a wrong assumption at the very base that they have your best interests in mind. In reality, most bosses are precisely the opposite. They are primarily interested in completing their work and advancing in their own careers. If you happen to be someone of utility to them, they will use your services. In many cases, they may be trying to work against your interests if that serves their purpose.

3. Your boss may sometimes be wholly incompetent and dangerous to your well-being: Some bosses are just inept. They manage to reach a position of importance due to several factors, such as bootlicking, luck, and connections. However, their basic incompetence remains unchanged, and no amount of effort from your side is going to change that fact. You need to accept their incompetence as fact and deal with them accordingly.

Let us understand this from the perspective of Sourav – a typical professional who does his work diligently and sticks to his routine.

Sourav was once under a boss who was highly incompetent in the tasks assigned to him. However, he used to rate himself very highly and always tried to shove his false sense of competence down Sourav's throat. He used to give completely wrong advice and directives at the drop of a hat. Thereafter, he used to dissociate himself from his own advice once it backfired.

Once Sourav studied him thoroughly, he understood that it was pointless to try and counter his advice and ideas in one-on-one discussions. Instead, Sourav understood that it was easier to dodge his ideas if they could be presented in group settings, such as review meetings or monthly meetings.

Sourav had another boss who harboured a great deal of covert rage and jealousy towards him. This was primarily due to two reasons, which Sourav understood over time, after keenly observing his behaviour and attitude.

(1) The boss was a covert narcissist: He was in a terrible marriage, which made him bitter all the time. That was worsened by the fact that Sourav's love life was going steadily.

(2) The boss considered himself to be an apostle of honesty and competency, and yet the organization did not believe him fit for several assignments. It used to bother him deeply when Sourav received any recognition for his professional competence.

What struck Sourav about this person was the variation in his attitude towards Sourav, depending on the issue at hand. So, if Sourav fared poorly in any of my assignments, he would commiserate and politely express the opinion that maybe he wasn't good enough for the job, and that he fully understood how it felt.

On other occasions, if Sourav were to ask for leave from the office to celebrate his anniversary, he would erupt in rage. If anyone praised Sourav in front of the boss, he would take out his rage later in a different task by intentionally highlighting Sourav's faults.

For a specific period, Sourav attempted to have both indirect and direct conversations with this person. It was essential for Sourav to convey that he had no enmity towards his boss, given his junior position in the hierarchy.

However, Sourav realised that the toxicity of this person made reaching a middle ground quite impossible. Sourav started maintaining a safe distance from him and only engaged with him on an absolutely-need-to-do basis. Soon afterwards, the boss left for a different company. Good riddance!

When it comes to building a relationship with your boss, it is crucial to maintain an open mind and assess the kind of person you are dealing with. The thumb rule is to maintain a professional distance with most of your bosses, unless you find a strong alignment of values and like-mindedness.

18.
Death of a Relationship

Many relationships deserve to die. This is a general principle that applies to many kinds of relationships, including professional, romantic, and friendly ones. While the start of most relationships is highly enthusiastic (new job, new spouse, new friend), their sustainability is primarily owed to the common sense and discipline to stick to basics. However, either or both of these factors are found wanting in many relationships, even after long periods of time. Such relationships, which often lack clarity, deserve to end quickly.

Let's face the fact – sometimes, despite our best efforts, we cannot fully control the type of people who come into our lives.

You may happen to be in an office where the boss or the next-door co-worker is an absolute misfit for developing a proper relationship with you. There is nothing you can really do if you discover that your boss is secretly having an affair with their assistant, and you happen to be a loyal partner. You cannot sermonize the boss into changing his ways. The aspect of changing people has already been discussed at length in a separate chapter. Neither can you forcibly change your own values and lifestyle to suit a misfiring professional relationship. At such times, it is advisable to establish strong boundaries, hold onto them at all times, and consider the relationship a lost cause when the sour aspects threaten to overwhelm your life.

Similarly, you need to be cautious when entering friendships that are not aligned with your value systems. Such friendships often cause long-term damage which cannot be undone even when the friend is no longer around. People who learn to smoke or drink as a matter of habit, from their "friend circles", go on spending truckloads of their hard-earned money on these habits. Friendship is an important relationship in life, and friends should be chosen with utmost care. However, we mostly end up befriending acquaintances we meet in common places, such as school, college, work, or the neighbourhood, and often end up in relationships with people who are fundamentally not aligned with us.

This is yet another truism of life – most of our so-called "friends" from school, college, or our first job vanish from our lives once the physical association ends. Consider this: How many of your friends from the past are really "in" your life, ever after, for significantly long periods of time?

Do you still have to face or have frequent conversations with the school bully who made you feel insecure about life? Most likely not, but if their influence on you was too strong in the past, it may have affected your mental well-being, which in turn may have had long-term consequences.

Do you still feel obligated to be in awe of the charming and over-the-top college batch-mate who influenced so many around them to try their first "hit" of narcotics? Most likely not, but if you managed to pick up the habit of taking drugs, it may have ruined your life in more ways than one.

Some people and the products of associating with them are not meant for us. Even though we may feel it within us when the association is ongoing, we tend to struggle with structuring our thought process to handle such associations and relationships.

Even though some unnecessary relationships tend to linger, what really stays with us in the long term are those that have a basic, foundational alignment between the people involved. Carrying the baggage of wrong friendships is a liability on life itself – we feel obligated to be in associations that don't align with our lives. That is not healthy in the long term.

Thus, while primary care should be taken in choosing the people that we allow into our lives, there should be greater introspection on the people we actually intend to keep in our lives. This does not mean that I am advocating a devilish hire-and-fire policy vis-à-vis relationships. Instead, it is recommended that we exercise due caution when allowing people into our lives.

If you move into a new home and your neighbour is an extrovert who loves to organize parties every other weekend, you need not adopt the same lifestyle just for the sake of social belongingness. If you are an introvert who loves to spend weekends reading on the couch, the new neighbour should not be able to make you feel awkward about it. If you are different from someone, you should establish boundaries that allow you to communicate these differences healthily.

A similar pattern of trying to fit in is visible across many schools and colleges, where "peer pressure" transforms young people into something they are not. This is because we struggle to cope with the baggage of past relationships at a young age. We tend to be overawed by people around us who are extroverted, charismatic or bullish.

If the most charismatic person in your college happens to ride a bike at 2 o'clock in the night, we feel that we are missing out on something if we are not able to do the same.

If the school topper whose newspaper interviews are a rave in your neighbourhood happens to be a pervert, it does not mean that you have to follow suit.

If your hostel mate enjoys gambling and his parents splurge their black money on him, you need not develop gambling habits or pressure your parents for more pocket money.

Being emotionally overwhelmed by people who are not right for us leads to a "herd mentality," where we tend to think and act in similar ways. This is a tragedy for human society when an individual stops developing and using the precious gift of the mind. It is due to the brilliance of the individual human mind that civilisation has progressed this far.

Just imagine what would have happened if Edison was influenced by a gambler friend to waste his life in gambling, debt and alcohol. How would global medicine have prospered if Louise Pasteur had not dedicated his life to the cause of betterment of human health and instead remained comfortable in his social circles? At the core of such examples lies the magic of independent thinking, which I have strongly endorsed throughout the book. As a matter of thumb rule, those relationships which degrade our capabilities for independent thinking deserve to end sooner or later.

Wrong relationships may not always be visible to the human eye, but they can profoundly affect our lives if we are not careful. This is why not every relationship deserves to be taken as a relationship. They have obvious expiry dates. Such relationships – whether with the wrong boss, the bully friend, the uncharacteristic girlfriend, or the nosy neighbour – should not have any lasting impact on our lives. Such an impact should be allowed to be created by the people with whom we can genuinely relate over long periods of time.

19.

Relationships: The Good, Bad, and Incentives

A natural extension to the chapter on life's unexciting aspects is the fact that most people tend to yearn for the positive aspects in a relationship and want to overlook any harmful elements. However, relationships are like stories in our life. Just like any other story that we read in a book or watch in a movie, there are always the good and bad sides coexisting.

It is difficult to find a good story where there is neither a hero nor a villain, or one where there is only a hero, with no adversary to challenge. Such stories, even if they exist, are most likely to be insipid and unrealistic. The same principle holds for any relationship – there will be both good and bad elements in it, and the dynamics will always be about enhancing and refining the positive aspects that benefit both sides. I have used the terms "good" and "bad" for simplicity of expression, but the issue is more nuanced than that.

In the case of romantic relationships, there will be issues that both sides agree with and encourage, and there will also be problems that both sides want to resolve over time. A relationship which appears to be entirely peaceful is abnormal and unrealistic. The same applies to professional relationships. There are likely to be technical and creative differences between individuals, even though they may share the same values and thought systems.

This is where the role of incentives comes in. If the baseline of a relationship is established, incentives can serve as the adhesive and motivation for both sides to work together to maintain the relationship and overcome the odds. However, it must be reiterated that for incentives to work correctly, the baseline or foundation of the relationship, formed through love, trust, empathy, and synergistic value systems, must be well established.

Consider your office. You may not like certain aspects of your job, such as office politics, the location of your cabin, or certain habits of your boss or colleagues. But does that mean you resign and go elsewhere just because you don't like those aspects? NO, because the work that you do earns you the remuneration, which in turn creates the systems which run your life. You would not be willing to upset the balance of your life on flimsy grounds. In this case, the salary you receive from your employer is a visible incentive that helps you stay committed to the job and try to work around the problematic issues. However, as already mentioned, this is presuming that you like the basic content of your job. If you hate data analysis and you have to earn a salary from a job where number crunching is the norm, the salary is not likely to soothe your misery for long.

Similarly, in the case of a marriage, if the partners are compatible at a fundamental level, they can navigate their way past thorny issues that arise from time to time, as these serve a useful purpose for both sides. At a very basic level, a marriage entails a division of labour and sharing of responsibilities. In the 21st century, we have moved far ahead of the narratives where the woman manages the household and the man earns the bread. Thus, sharing of responsibilities has become more nuanced. Women, instead of just being homemakers, are nowadays more active in sharing the financial burden of a household. Financial burden getting shared between husband and wife usually means a better standard of living, which is a win-win situation for both.

While this is a tangible incentive, the intangible ones also deserve mention. Emotional security comes with a high premium these days – if you are with someone you can trust, you feel emotionally secure in times of stress and anxiety. The same is true of your partner, who trusts you and believes that her support shall be reciprocated when needed. Such emotional security is a valuable asset in life, as most people discover over time. However, it is equally challenging to earn and manage and requires hard work over time.

The same logic applies to most other forms of relationships as well, such as siblings, friends, and neighbours. If the basic elements are compatible, relationships tend to evolve as incentives are negotiated and the benefits of cooperation are understood. The mistake people make is that they either waste time in relationships whose fundamentals are missing or they are not patient enough with fundamentally sound relationships, simply because the incentives are not immediately visible.

Conclusion

Human relationships form the core of our society. Without strong relationships, which are held together by proper dynamics, it is impossible to have a stable and prosperous society. The most fundamental relationship for a human being begins within their family, parents, siblings, and other immediate family members. As one ages, the relationships widen and more people may come into the picture, spouse, children, professional colleagues and bosses, neighbours, etc.

A person with the right mindset about relationships generally manages to handle most of their relationships well enough. On the other hand, someone whose basic understanding of human relationships is flawed in some way always finds it difficult to build long-lasting, productive relationships in life. People who have experienced difficult relationships of any kind in their lives need to draw the proper lessons from such relationships. The right lessons improve their lives in the long run, while the wrong lessons only push them into a larger maze of sub-optimal relationships.

Good relationships act as force multipliers in life. They help you prosper in the long run. Bad relationships tend to have the opposite effect. They scuttle your chances of making it big in life, even if you are oozing with natural talent. This is why learning the art of handling relationships is one of the major components of growing up and maturing as a human being. Without mastering this art, it is well-nigh impossible to succeed or have a meaningful life in any way.

Acknowledgements

Writing about relationships is one thing. Writing an entire book about relationships is quite another. The way I feel and think about human relationships is primarily because I tend to observe people, events and narratives in multiple dimensions. My observations have been primarily built on the foundation of good schooling and strong parenting.

Parents and school, two of my earliest and closest forms of human association, were the foundational relationships of my life, which taught me the skills of observation and comprehension.

I am thankful to my parents for instilling in me the concept of love, human bonding and relationships in a subtle and meaningful way. I had an exceptional childhood by many standards, even though I grew up in an average middle-class household. It sounds easy to portray parents in divine light, but exceptional parents are actually pretty difficult to find!

I am thankful to my school, St. Xavier's Durgapur, for setting the priorities correctly in my childhood. The school provided me with an exceptional set of teachers to learn from and a congenial environment in which to grow. I may not have achieved much professional success without the foundation laid during my school days.

I also thank the friends who betrayed me in some way, women who may have spurned my proposals, and professional colleagues and bosses who may have backstabbed me. These experiences motivated me to write a book and lend a helping hand to those who may be struggling to handle the relationships in their lives.

Suggested Reading

Dweck, Carol S. Mindset: *The New Psychology of Success*. New York: Random House, 2006.

Pink, Daniel H. Drive: *The Surprising Truth* about What Motivates Us. New York: Riverhead Books, 2009.

Duckworth, Angela. *Grit: The Power of Passion and Perseverance*. New York: Scribner, 2016.

Acemoglu, Daron, and James A. Robinson. *Why Nations Fail: The Origins of Power, Prosperity, and Poverty*. New York: Crown Business, 2012.

Harari, Yuval Noah. *Sapiens: A Brief History of Humankind*. New York: Harper, 2015.

Clear, James. Atomic Habits: *An Easy & Proven Way to Build Good Habits & Break Bad Ones*. New York: Avery, 2018.

Cain, Susan. Quiet: *The Power of Introverts in a World That Can't Stop Talking*. New York: Crown Publishers, 2012.

Sandel, Michael J. *What Money Can't Buy: The Moral Limits of Markets*. New York: Farrar, Straus and Giroux, 2012.

Rotella, Bob. *How Champions Think: In Sports and in Life*. New York: Simon & Schuster, 2015.

Housel, Morgan. *The Psychology of Money: Timeless Lessons on Wealth, Greed, and Happiness*. Harriman House, 2020.

Housel, Morgan. *Same as Ever: A Guide to What Never Changes*. Harriman House, 2023.

Sutton, Nicholas. *The Power of Dharma: An Introduction to Hinduism and Vedic Philosophy*. CreateSpace Independent Publishing, 2017.

Hollins, Peter. *Mental Models: 30 Thinking Tools That Separate the Average from the Exceptional*. PH Learning International, 2019.

Sinek, Simon. *Leaders Eat Last: Why Some Teams Pull Together and Others Don't*. New York: Portfolio/Penguin, 2014.

Nguyen, Joseph. *Don't Believe Everything You Think: Why Your Thinking Is the Beginning and End of Suffering*. One Satori, 2022.

Jorgenson, Eric, ed. *The Almanack of Naval Ravikant: A Guide to Wealth and Happiness*. San Francisco: Magrathea Publishing, 2020.

Watts, Alan. *The Wisdom of Insecurity: A Message for an Age of Anxiety*. New York: Pantheon, 1951.

Durvasula, Ramani. *It's Not You: Identifying and Healing from Narcissistic People*. New York: Penguin Life, 2023.

Epictetus. *The Art of Living: The Classical Manual on Virtue, Happiness, and Effectiveness*. Translated by Sharon Lebell. New York: HarperOne, 1995.

Mirza, Debbie. *The Covert Passive-Aggressive Narcissist: Recognizing the Traits and Finding Healing after Hidden Emotional and Psychological Abuse*. Debbie Mirza Publishing, 2017.

Hardy, Darren. *The Compound Effect: Jumpstart Your Income, Your Life, Your Success*. New York: Vanguard Press, 2010.